China: Its Most Scenic Places

China: Its Most Scenic Places

A Photographic Journey through 50 of
Its Most Unspoiled Villages and Towns

Reader's
Digest

THE READER'S DIGEST ASSOCIATION, INC.
Pleasantville, New York/Montreal/Hong Kong

A READER'S DIGEST BOOK

Copyright © 2005 The Reader's Digest Association, Inc.

U.S. Project Editor: Marcy Gray
Editorial Consultant: Nancy Shuker
Project Designer: George McKeon, Yiping Yang
Executive Editors, Trade Publishing: Dolores York, Longgen Chen, Ying Wu
Art Designers: Sally Chen, Loretta Loh
Illustrations: Loretta Loh
Cover Design: Sally Chen
Picture Research: Willy Xu
Associate Publisher, Trade Publishing: Christopher T. Reggio
President & Publisher, Trade Books and Music Group: Harold Clarke

This book was edited and designed by Reader's Digest Association Far East
Limited, in partnership with Shanghai Literature & Art Publishing House and
Shanghai Press & Publishing Development Company.

Library of Congress Cataloging-in-Publication Data

China: Its Most Scenic Places: A photographic journey through 50 of its most
unspoiled villages and towns / Reader's Digest
        p. cm.
Includes index.
ISBN 0-7621-0620-4
1. China Pictorial works. I. Reader's Digest Association.

DS706.3.C463 2005
915.1'0022'2–dc22
                                    2004061422
Address any comments about China: Its Most Scenic Places to:
        The Reader's Digest Association, Inc.
        Adult Trade Publishing
        Reader's Digest Road
        Pleasantville, NY 10570-7000

For more Reader's Digest products and information, visit our website:
        www.rd.com (in the United States)

Printed in China

1 3 5 7 9 10 8 6 4 2

Introduction

China is one of the world's oldest civilizations, and while it has a number of highly developed urban centers, it also plays host to a wide variety of wild and unspoiled sites of astounding natural beauty.

CHINA: ITS MOST SCENIC PLACES explores more than 50 of the country's most beautiful villages and towns. Whether you'd like to explore these places in person or use this book as an armchair travel guide, you'll discover Chinese life as it has gone on for many centuries. You'll visit a variety of landscapes, from a Hunan village set among peach orchards—its admirers have claimed that this is a famous Jin Dynasty bard's fairy-tale retreat among the peach blossoms—to the ancient ruins of the Stone City on the Silk Road. You'll travel from the dense forests of the Little White Mountains in the northeast to the Tibetan grasslands and from the rugged Altai Mountains in the northwest to the terraced fields of southern China. Tourist maps included for each of the villages and towns will show you where a site is located.

And as you flip through this guide's breathtaking photos, you'll gain a better understanding of the culture of this ancient land and the treasures that it holds. You'll see, for example, a town where horse-drawn sleighs are the popular—and sometimes the only—transportation in the winter and the traditional festival costumes of women in the Miaoling mountain range. This off-the-beaten path journey through China's most scenic places offers you a rare glimpse of secluded areas that are vital to the country's vast population. It brings you into close contact with the life of the Dong and Buyi in southern China; it takes you into the Hakka earth towers and the Huizhou-style houses; it shows you the distinct campfire dances of the Tibetans, the annual Water Festival of the Shui people, the Dongba culture of the Naxi and the matriarchal society of the Musuo. Share the joys and experience the life of the Chinese with CHINA: ITS MOST SCENIC PLACES.

Contents

The Northern Region

8-37

The Western Region

38-103

The Central Region

104-187

188-245

The Southern Region

The Northern Region

Snow Country
in the Little White Mountains

The Little White Mountain Range, or Zhangguang-cai Ling in Chinese, is located in Heilongjiang, China's most northern province. This range is part of a huge area of mountainous terrain that includes the Changbai Shan (Ever White Mountain). These heavily forested mountains supply China with much of its timber. The Northeast, also called dongbei, is home to the Manchurian people who have a long history in the area. Archaeological discoveries verify that this region was inhabited for at least 4,000 years. During the Qing Dynasty when Manchu emperors ruled all of China, the royal family made ritual journeys to the mountains of the Northeast. Sometimes they went to Zhangguangcai Ling with its excellent feng shui, instead of making the arduous trip to Sky Lake up Changbai Shan for the ritual tribute to the heavens. Even with the immense resources of the imperial treasury, an annual trip to the highest elevations in the Changbai Shan might have been impossible due to the Northeast's harsh climate and long winters with snow on the ground at high elevations most of the year.

A cozy mountain home blanketed by snow in the Snow Country (below). Horse-drawn sleighs are a popular and, in some areas, the only transportation in the winter (opposite).

There are still areas of primeval forest in Zhangguangcai Ling—vast forests of pine, white birch, spruce and maple—that are home to the black bear, boar, roe deer and fox. Deep in the mountains, far from most settlements, loggers and their families live a life rare in China. Visitors in the past might have avoided the severe winter months in these mountains, but a ski resort is now a major attraction that takes advantage of the heavy snowfalls. This area of the mountains at Shuang-

feng Lingchang (Twin Peak Logging Farm) on the southwestern slopes of Zhangguangcai Ling is appropriately called the Snow Country. During the short summer, visitors can explore the remains of the city of Wula, built at least 600 years ago. Wula was once inhabited by one of the area's ethnic tribes called the Jurchen. There are also two well-known hot springs and two lovely rivers, the Hailang He and Erdaohai, which all together create a pristine area for recreation in the Northeast.

Deep winter snows last for up to eight months in this region, keeping houses (opposite) and roads (above) covered in snow.

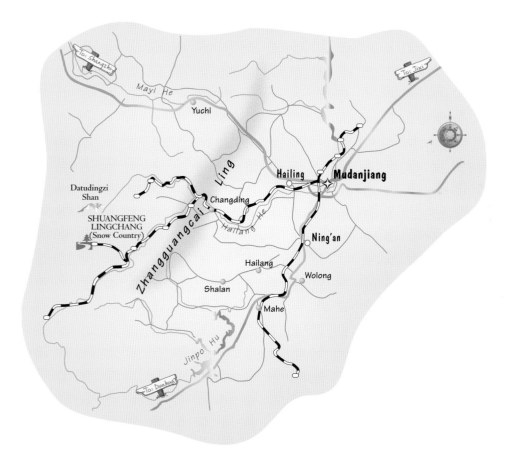

Changbai Shan

The province of Jilin in northeast China is closer to Korea than most of the rest of China. The Changbai Shan (Ever White Mountain) in Jilin is part of this area characterized by long severe winters, and so the name suits this snowy range. Formed by volcanic action, the mountains are the largest range in northeast China and have a number of tall peaks over 8,000 ft. (2,400 m). Three major rivers in the area cut through the mountain range, the Tumen, the Songhua and the river that marks the border between China and Korea, the Yalu. Dense forest covers much of the area, and today China's largest nature reserve protects the eighty types of trees and some three hundred medicinal plant species found in this remote region. A number of conifers native to the area and the rare Changbai larch that thrive in wintry temperatures are found in the forests of this beautiful mountain range. The extensive area contains a great range of elevations with related flora and fauna in lush forests at about 3,000 ft. (900 m) to treeless windswept expanses above 6,000 ft. (1,800 m).

It was from this mountain range, along with the entire northern area of China, that the last ruling

Cultivated ginseng are grown in an area rich in wild medicinal plants (above). Winter winds in the Changbai Shan whip the high peaks around Tianchi (opposite).

dynasty, the Qing, arrived in Beijing in 1644 and established its capital. The Qing rulers guarded their stronghold and declared Changbai Shan off-limits to outsiders. The medicinal plants of this snowy mountain range, especially ginseng, were reputed to be among the finest in China.

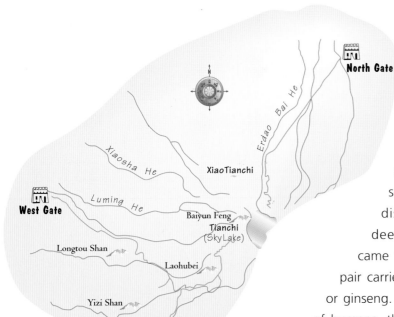

Three Treasures

This area has a charming folk legend to describe the origin of the three treasures of northeast China: sable fur, ginseng and the sika deer. The story goes that the son and daughter of a dragon king disguised themselves as two sika deer, and with the help of a sable came to visit the world of humans. The pair carried with them the longevity flower, or ginseng. In his eagerness to visit the world of humans, the boy had carelessly forgotten to hide his dragon horns under his disguise. Later, in a panic that they might be recognized, they fled the world of humans leaving the longevity flower, the boy's dragon-shaped horns, which all sika deer have, and the sable, the bearer of luxurious fur.

Tianchi

One of China's most beautiful lakes is part of this mountain range. Tianchi, or Sky Lake is located in an ancient volcanic cone near the top of one of these peaks. At over 7,000 ft. (2,100 m) in elevation, Tianchi is frequently swathed in mist. But when conditions are right the reflection of the sixteen peaks that surround the

The banks of Tianchi (Sky Lake) are covered with alpine flowers in the summer.

lake is breathtaking. The lake is also the source for the Songhua River. To the north side of the lake there is an opening where the lake water spills over to form a mile-long Chengcha River before it drops over a vertical cliff into the Second White River, the main tributary of the Songhua River.

THE GREAT GORGE

It was not until a 1987 storm in the Changbai Shan region that a previously unknown gorge over 490 ft. (150 m) deep was discovered in the western part of the range. Changbai Shan Nature Reserve staff were on an expedition to assess the storm damage when they stumbled on this hidden stretch of the Jinjiang River that runs through the gorge, carved over time by the slow and steady action of the river winding its course through lava rock in this ancient volcanic range. Many bizarre rock formations are part of the gorge, and though some have been named, others wait for an inspired observer to find a fitting title. Lush and green, the crystal-clear water, ancient trees and rare species of plants make this beautiful gorge another wonder of this mountainous border area of northeast China.

There is much more in these mountains including springs, lakes and great forests with rich plant and animal life. There are also a number of hot springs with temperatures up to 180°F (82°C). These springs contain hydrogen sulfide, believed to have medicinal value, that draws visitors to their comforting warmth.

There are two entrances to the Changbai Shan Nature Reserve. The Great Gorge can be reached from the West Gate.

The *White* Rivers

The Changbai Shan range, which runs approximately north and south, takes up much of the province of Jilin from Dalian in the south to the Russian border in the north. The Songhua River that begins in the western slopes of the range runs a course that takes it northwest through China's most northern province of Heilongjiang where it joins the Amur River, the Russian name for the Heilongjiang, or Black Dragon River that forms the border between Russia and China.

When visiting Changbai Shan, the southwestern side of the range has much to offer, though the northern side has always been more accessible. There the tributaries of the Songhua River have been conveniently named by number as the First and Second White rivers, or Toudao and Erdao Bai He in Chinese. The region has a number of historic sites and relics that may have survived in part because their remote location protected them. Near the First White River there is an ancient pagoda thought to have been built during the Liao Reign about one thousand years ago on Pagoda Hill.

The rare Meiren Song (pines) are found only in the White Rivers region.

This is called the Pagoda of the Sacred Light because it is believed it could have only survived with the protection of sacred lights. There are also the remains of a Ming Dynasty city called Treasure Horse City. Unfortunately, the buildings are entirely gone, but fragments of the city wall still exist in this beautiful setting.

It is also the only area where Meiren Song (opposite) is found. Meaning "beauty pine" in Chinese, it is a pine tree of the Pinus Sylvestris family, known for its tall elegance like a beautiful lady, hence the name. The seasons are varied in this mountainous region: cool springs give way to scorching summer heat, followed by spec-tacular autumn colors, and winters with sub-zero temperatures. The best time to visit may be the spring and fall when temperatures are more moderate, although winter in the mountains is a season of great beauty. It's a time when the region sleeps under a deep blanket of snow. For the intrepid visitor this watershed area of the Songhua River has its own beauty year round.

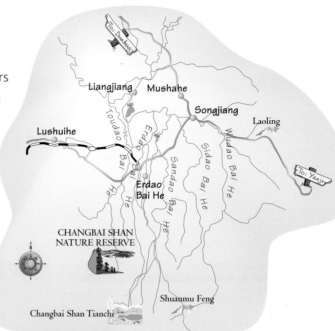

The sparkling Second White River flows past a home in the Changbai Shan region.

Yanbian, Home for the Ethnic Koreans

In China's northeast, the province of Jilin has an unusual border area where China's Tumen Jiang (River) empties into the Sea of Japan. There, a narrow strip of land provides China access to the sea. North Korea is to the south, Russia to the north, and from the small coastal town of Fangchuan, a sweeping view of North Korea, Russia and a glimpse of Japan can be seen on a clear day.

This hilly region has a large ethnic Korean population of over forty percent. Beautifully green in the spring and summer and dotted with fertile fields, this region of China has been off the beaten track for visitors; as a result, it remains a fascinating example of quiet countryside in the most heavily forested province of China. In the city of Yanji, the capital of the prefecture, most residents speak both Korean and Mandarin. The capital seat is a convenient location for exploring this unusual part of northeast China.

A relaxing option when visiting Yanbian is to explore by train. The slow pace allows for a leisurely tour of the area. Travelers will find Korean culture on display in Yanbian especially during festivals such as the New Year, Dragon Boat and Mid-Autumn, with a decidedly Korean flavor. Local villagers can be seen in brightly colored dress celebrating with Korean folk songs and dances that have been preserved in this area. A Korean instrument called the jiaye zither accompanied by drums and flutes is often used to provide the music.

The cuisine of the region is hearty, and one of the best-known dishes, now popular well beyond the Northeast, is the dumpling, or jiaozi. Made with an endless variety of fillings, the jiaozi can be eaten boiled, steamed or fried. A big bowl of jiaozi makes a delicious meal all by itself. Korean noodles are another staple made in the Korean style with the noodles served cold in a broth with tasty tidbits and spicy accompaniments. Kimchee, the famous Korean pickled cabbage, appears at almost every meal. Kimchee's fiery heat is due to the generous addition of chili peppers, a necessity in Korean cooking. Although it can be found in other parts of

A typical winter scene of the Yanbian forest (opposite).

China, dog meat may be on the menu also. It is said to be especially warming and is popular in the winter months.

The Yanbian region has been shaped by its unique geographical location. Today a visit to Yanbian is an opportunity to combine historic sites with unspoiled country life far from the bustle of large cities. It is not uncommon to see traditional wooden houses with

Traditional Korean-style houses in Yanbian with thatched roofs (below). The remote village of Fangchuan (opposite) borders on North Korea and Russia, connected by a railway bridge over the Tumen Jiang.

thatched roofs built in the Korean style. The village of Hongqi outside of Yanji is a particularly good example of this fast disappearing style. A summer cruise on the Tumen Jiang, a river that borders China and North Korea, is another great way to see the area, and it brings the visitor through a green landscape of mountains covered with verdant forests. The brilliantly colored jindalai, a wildflower native to the area, makes spring an ideal time to visit for those who love nature.

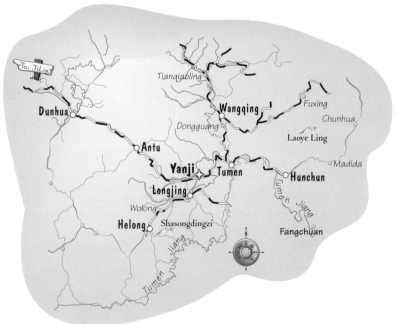

The *Yiwulü* Mountains

The beauty and importance of mountains is an ancient theme in the history of China. Mention of the Yiwulü Mountains in the northeast Liaoning Province goes back more than 2,000 years to a text titled *The Book of Courtesy* of the Zhou Dynasty. In this book, written during the early period of Chinese civilization, the Yiwulü Mountains are listed as one of the five groups of mountains guarding China, an honored status that this range of peaks still deserves. Although not the highest of the mountains in China, the area has long played a part in history. Certainly another of the indicators of importance in China is the numerous names applied to these mountains by various writers.

The Yiwulü Mountains, revered by both scholars and emperors of successive Chinese dynasties, were favorites of the Manchu conquerors from the northeast of China who established the Qing Dynasty. The Manchu emperors made an annual visit to the Yiwulü Mountains to pay tribute as part of their expeditions east to offer sacrifices to their ancestors.

A common expression of appreciation of natural

An elaborately carved memorial pagoda in Yiwulü.

beauty among the elite of China was to write poetry and comparisons of one mountain to other famous mountains in China, and the Yiwulü Mountains have many examples of this literary praise. Emperors often built pavilions and temples in places of outstanding beauty and inspiration. The Yiwulü Mountains still have a number of these elegant creations hidden in the pines and cypress that grow in this region. Today the Yiwulü are part of a nature reserve in Liaoning Province. Visitors will still be able to locate more than fifty royal inscriptions that are evidence of the lasting admiration generations have had for these lovely mountains.

An elegant pavilion frames the view of the Yiwulü Mountains.

Hulun Buir
Grassland

In the northeast corner of Inner Mongolia, near the Russian border, a vast sea of green extends as far as you can see in the summer. This is the Hulun Buir Grassland (above), a pristine prairie of tall grasses, dotted with lakes and more than one thousand rivers and small streams. The grassland is named for its two major lakes: Hulun and Buir, believed in local legend to have been formed by the tears of two young Mongolian lovers after they had been separated by evil forces. From late June to mid-August, wildflowers mix with the grasses in a dazzling display of colors.

The Hulun Buir Grassland was a cradle of nomadic life in northern China. Archaeological evidence of tools, such as stone arrows and bone knives, as well as skull fossils, suggests human habitation as early as 10,000 years ago. Later, ancient nomads of the Xianbei (Sien-pi), Kitan, Jurchen and Mongol tribes settled here, leaving behind simple but elegant earthenware and bronze pots. First taking root in the Argun River basin, the Mongols began in the middle of the eighth century to rove around the area near the Onon, Kerulun and Heilongjiang (Amur) rivers. In the eleventh century, they moved back to the Hulun Buir Grassland. Here, where rich plant life easily sustained both men and herds, Genghis Khan began to develop his military power.

The Hulun Buir Grassland today includes meadows, forest prairie and steppes. The land supports thousands of species of plants and more than four hundred animals and birds. Sanhe cows—famous for their prolific milk production—graze here. And so do Sanhe horses, famous for their physical stamina.

The southwest corner of the grassland is the northeastern edge of the Mongolian Plateau, flat and extensive, like an enormous emerald carpet. The terrain to the west of Lake Hulun is similar in topography to the northeast part of the grassland, but it is more arid and supports fewer grasses.

There are some 540 lakes in the Hulun Buir plain. The largest are Hulun Nur and Buir Nur, which are linked by the Orxon Gol (River). Hulun Nur, or Hulun Lake (also called Chalai Nor or Dalai Nor), is the fifth largest lake in China. It is 50 miles (80 km) long and 22 miles (35 km)

Natural habitat is well-preserved along the Jiliu He (River) to the north of Hulun Buir Grassland.

Mukeleng refers to simple log houses once built in the Hailaer area with a distinct Russian style.

wide, with a maximum depth of 26 ft. (8 m). Fed by the Kolulun (or Herlen) Gol from the South-west and the Hulun River from the East, its water level and quality fluctuate frequently from deep freshwater to shallow, slightly salty water. The lake is home to many different species of fish, as well as such birds as ospreys, teals, swans, wild geese and cranes. Reeds and duckweeds grow around the lake. The lakeside area is also rich in underground minerals. Beautiful agate stones used to be found almost everywhere.

Buir Nur (Lake) to the south of Hulun Lake covers an

area of 235 sq. miles (609 sq. km) with a maximum depth of 33 ft. (10 m). The Ha-lo-hsin River feeds this freshwater lake from the Southeast, and the lake, in turn, feeds the Orxon Gol that flows into Hulun Lake to the North. In the last year of Kublai Khan's Yuan Dynasty (1368), Emperor Shun was chased by one of Zhu Yuangzhang's generals to the lake, which witnessed both the rise and fall of the Yuan Dynasty. Zhu later became the first emperor of the Ming Dynasty.

Hailaer, the old capital city of Hulun Buir, was built on the left bank of the Yimin He (River) in 1732 as a defense against the Russians. With two rivers, the Yimin

Mor Gol (left) is one of the thousands of rivers that flow through the heart of the Hulun Buir Grassland. White yurts are pitched to provide lodging for the visitors to Hulun Buir (below).

and Hailaer, running through the town, the city attracted throngs of both Chinese and Russian merchants to its markets. Even today, Mongolian yurts are interspersed with Russian-style houses. Herdsmen and businessmen of many ethnic groups still come from all around the region to this busy northern city.

Traveling westward along the Hailaer He, one reaches the city of Manzhouli (or Manchurie) on the border between China and Russia. Manzhouli has long served as a hub for transport to Russia and Central Europe. More Russian-style wood and stone houses can be seen here, mixed with Chinese style buildings.

In spite of its fertile land, the Hulun Buir Grassland is sparsely populated. Mongolians, the original inhabitants

Architectural style of the buildings in the border town, Manzhouli, reflects distinct Russian influence.

of the region, still raise their herds here. They live in circular domed tents, called yurts, and their staple foods are meat and dairy products, which are commonly referred to as "red foods" and "white foods." It is the land of five animals—sheep, goats, cattle, horses and camels. The main meat is mutton, though camel meat and beef are also popular. White foods include yogurt, milk tea, and milk wine as well as cheese, cream, milk curd and milk cakes. Mongolians are a hospitable people. When visitors come, the hostess will hurry off to prepare milk cakes, while the host will hand over his snuff bottle to his guests for a try. Mongolians accompany their songs with a stringed instrument called a matouqin, which has a scroll carved like a horse's head.

The traditional Mongolian sports festival is called Naadam and features wrestling matches, archery contests and horse and camel races. The festivals are usually held in the late summer.

Wrestling matches are one of the features of the traditional Mongolian Naadam.

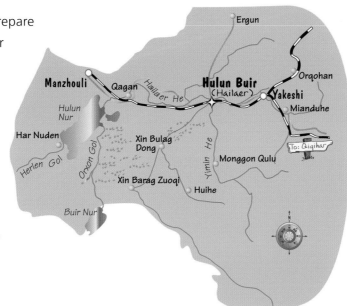

Alxa, Home of Bactrian Camels

Alxa, an area in the extreme western part of Inner Mongolia, is the natural semi-desert home of Bactrian camels, the ones with two humps. Alxa herdsmen depend on these camels for their livelihood. Camels can live on thorny herbal or woody shrubs and survive very well in desolate desert that would defeat other animals. They can tolerate extremely hot weather and go without water or food for five to six days, even under the sun. Weighing an average of 880 lb. (400 kg), a camel can carry a load of 440 lb. (200 kg) and travel 12 to 25 miles (20 to 40 km) a day.

The Bactrian camel is a multipurpose animal, mainly used for riding, hauling loads and producing wool, meat and milk. Camels are the only means of transport in Alxa; calling them "boats of the desert" is appropriate here. Camel meat is eaten and even the skin of a dead camel has all the uses of leather. Camels are very important in the high plains, deserts and semi-deserts of north and northwest China.

The Badan Jilin sand dunes are a beauty to behold (opposite), and the Bactrian camels (right) are well adapted to the dry desert.

About a third of the Alxa region–104,248 sq. miles (270,000 sq. km)–is desert, but that ratio is increasing at an alarming rate of over 386 sq. miles (1,000 sq. km) a year. The causes include reduced rainfall, over-browsing by herds of camels, goats and other animals as well as a growing population. The water table under Alxa has been pumped dry and the air is very dry. A quarter of the sand in the terrible storms that sweep over China every spring comes from the Alxa Desert.

The sand sea that the "boats of the desert" sail through is as tough and unpredictable as the deep blue sea. The Badan Jilin Desert in Alxa is made up of crescent-shaped moving sand dunes. Some of the dunes are linked to each other, appearing like a chain locking the desert, others look like huge pyramids up to 1,600 ft. (500 m) high. Numerous inland lakes that the local herdsmen call haizi are scattered among the sand dunes, surrounded by oases with luxuriant grasses.

With the expansion of desert, many historical relics in the Alxa area have been submerged in sand, including the ruins of Heicheng (Black City). Situated in the Ejin Qi (or Banner) at the edge of the Badan Jilin Desert, Heicheng was the ancient capital of the state of Western Xia. The Yanfu Monastery was built there during the reign of Emperor Yongzheng of the Qing Dynasty (1644–1911) as an ancestral temple for a royal family. The architectural style was elegant, and the Buddha statues were finely carved. Much of the structure is gone. What remains are the front gate, the main hall, and the east and west side halls.

The ruins of the Black City (opposite) are more than half buried by the sand dunes, while diversiform-leaf poplars (below) struggle to survive the extremely dry desert.

Diversiform-leaf poplars are regarded as a living fossil, having been around for about three million years. In early 2004 a poplar forest park was created in Ejin Banner to protect the species from extinction.

The Western Region

The *Altai* Mountains

Bordering Xinjiang, far to the northwest of China, the Altai Mountains are part of a much larger range that spread from southern Siberia in Russia to the Gobi Desert. Most of this remote and lovely range of mountains is wild and uninhabited. In eastern Asia the Altai are the last great range of mountains before they change from the arid steppes of Mongolia to the endless stretches of coniferous forest called taiga that circle the northern hemisphere on both the European and Asian continents. Further north the taiga gives way to Arctic tundra. The Mongolian Altai Mountains range in height from 9,000–14,350 ft. (2,750–4,374 m), and have only recently begun to draw intrepid climbers looking for another challenging peak to scale. Hundreds of mountain glaciers feed rivers and lakes to the north and south of the Altai range, including one of the great rivers of Siberia, the Ob, that travels north 3,362 miles (5,410 km) to finally empty into the Arctic Ocean. On the southern side of the range, countless mountain streams

The Crescent Moon Bay (left) in Kanas Lake, lies serenely in the Altai forests. Downstream the Hemu River runs through the beautiful Burqin countryside (opposite).

converge to form the Ulungur He, a continental river, and the Ertix He that eventually turns northward to become the only river in China that flows all the way to the Arctic.

There is amazing plant diversity in the Altai Mountains. Huge expanses of subtropical deciduous trees, conifers such as pine and fir, and European spruce and white birch thrive at different elevations. Wildflowers bloom throughout much of the year from the lower slopes to far up the mountains in high, rocky crevices where sparse, sandy soil near the snow line supports the Tianshan Snow Lotus, famous for its pale, translucent petals and large purple center characteristic of the lotus family. In this remote mountain wilderness, its unique ecosystem protected from disturbance, birds such as the golden eagle continue to live in peace. The Altai is one of the few places in Asia that still claims the snow leopard among its residents, plus many other wild creatures.

The lower slopes and the nearby rich grasslands of the Altai region are home to scattered communities of Mongolians and Kazaks who still lead semi-nomadic lives. The Kazak people graze large herds of sheep and camels in the rich foothills. In the Turkic language of the

Dusty red rocks glow under the setting sun in Altai (left). The local herdsmen take their livestock from one pastureland to another (above).

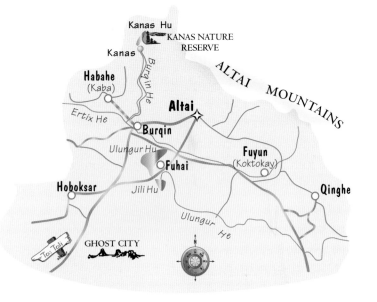

local Mongolian people, the Altai Mountains are called "the gold mountains." There is an old saying that there are seventy-two gullies in the Altai and there is gold in every one. It may be true, but today the Altai Mountains retain something infinitely more valuable: the beauty and diversity of a great mountain wilderness that all the Altai gold could never buy.

KANAS LAKE

The icy waters of the Kanas Glacier in the Altai Mountains fill the North Kanas River, and are the source of the crystal-clear Kanas Hu (Lake), also known as Hanas Lake. This shining gem nestles in the Altai Mountains at an elevation of 4,508 ft. (1,374 m). Its attractive scenic setting has frequently been compared to the alpine landscape of Switzerland. About fifteen miles (24 km) long and over a mile (1.9 km) wide, it is

the second deepest lake in China at 618 ft. (189 m). Kanas Lake teems with fish. Especially noteworthy are a species of landlocked salmon local people call the big red fish. Some of them are said to grow to nearly 50 ft. (15 m) in length. Fanciful tales of horses and camels falling into the lake and being eaten by these huge lake monsters are told with relish by local residents.

The lake has a number of bays created by streams that flow into it. Visitors are especially keen to view Wolongwan or Sleeping Dragon Bay (opposite) and Yueliangwan or Crescent Moon Bay that resemble their namesakes. The Sleeping Dragon is formed by a sandy island in Kanas Lake in the shape of a dragon, while a crescent-shaped section of the lake spectacularly turns from dark green to bright blue and milky white just as do other parts of the lake depending on the light.

THE TUWA VILLAGES

The Kanas Nature Reserve includes a number of Tuwa villages (see photo of a Tuwa village in Habahe County, pages 46–47). Although the people are considered Mongolian, their language is closer to the Kazak language. The Tuwa people have managed to preserve their ancient way of life as nomadic herdsmen, living in wooden houses with pointed roofs.

Evidence of human habitation in the Altai region can be found in cave paintings, and carved figures that date back two to three thousand years. Scenes of herding, hunting, battle and dancing illustrate the life of early nomadic ancestors who found the Altai as appealing long ago as the Tuwa do today.

The Mysterious and Magical Ghost City

Near the northwest edge of one of China's driest regions, the Junggar Basin in Xinjiang, is a city only in name. The 12-sq.-mile (31-sq.-km) Ghost City is nature's uncanny attempt to build a metropolis of rock carved by the forces of wind and water over millions of years. The scientific name for the peculiar terrain—Yadan Topography—comes from the Uygur word meaning steep mounds. The local Mongolian and Kazak herdsmen supplied the name Ghost City since they have heard the ghostly cries that echo through the empty "city" during the strong winds of spring and fall.

Visitors to the Ghost City are amazed by what appears at first glance to be lanes and streets, but on closer inspection are the patterns of erosion on what was once a plateau. A vast network of small valleys, hills, ditches and gullies stretches for miles. But this is not what is truly remarkable about the area. Strange shapes populate this ghost town's streets and byways. Some rocks

Ghostly echoes cry through a "city" carved by the wind and rain.

look like magnificent, ancient palaces. There seem to be places for worship cut from stone such as Buddhist pagodas and mosques with domes. Other places seem meant for wandering and dreaming in pavilions and gazebos in some long ago garden. The Ghost City also has its share of monuments to the brave and powerful in the shape of pyramids, and the city has protection in its rocks resembling military forts and strongholds.

On a sunny day the city has no hint of ghostly terrors, and visitors are completely swept up in the challenge of identifying the castles, palaces and architectural shapes, which hint at buildings that might never have existed except in the imagination of the beholder of this beautiful work of nature. There are places that do seem threatening simply because of massive boulders atop that might tumble down. But soon attention switches to the ground the visitor walks on. In many places it is scattered with bright pebbles of brilliant red, glistening black and jadelike ivory. Once in a while agates can be found

A seasonal pond in the Ghost City (opposite). Dinosaurs once roamed this part of the earth (top).

among this unusual carpet of stone.

The Ghost City, painted in the yellows, browns and reds of the area's soil, is set off by another work of nature that glistens black in the strong sunlight of this desert landscape. Nearly 25 miles (40 km) of naturally occurring asphalt unwinds like a ribbon through the rolling hills of the area. Beyond the Ghost City the entire region is full of interesting sites to explore. Urho, a desert oasis in the same general area, is a spectacular botanical garden of oasis plants. Poplars, red willows and bulrushes line the creeks and streams. Not far from the oasis is Elik Hu (or Ailike Lake), which has recently revived after a ten-year disappearance. Another lake full of glistening salt deposits is used for producing saltpeter and niter. Dinosaurs once lived in the Junggar Basin when the region was temperate, and the fossils of these great creatures are gathered and studied in this driest of China's lands.

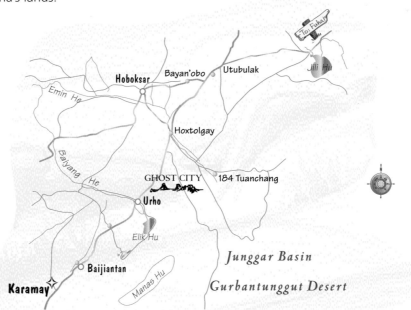

The *Ili* River Valley

The vast Ili River Valley is one of the few locations in Xinjiang, China's largest western provincial region, that is not a desert. Shielded by the large Tian Shan (Sky Mountains) Range on the south and the much smaller Borohoro Shan Range on the north, the valley is protected from frigid Siberian winds and the dry winds and sand storms of the Taklimakan Desert. Warm, moist air currents from further east also play a vital part in the rainfall the valley needs to support the dense forests and beautiful grasslands of this unusual inland region. The impressive varieties of wild grass in the Ili River Valley have yet to be identified completely. To date, 270 types of grass have been cataloged, over 100 of which were found to have medicinal uses.

The Ili He (River) begins far to the northwest in a large lake in Kazakhstan. During some of its course eastward it forms the border between China and Kazakhstan. When it finally enters the Ili River Valley, it flows nearly 900 miles (1,500 km) along the valley floor, fed by the tributaries of the Künes and Tekes rivers. It ends its jour-

The verdant Ili River Valley is considered a land of abundance, suitable for both farming and animal husbandry.

ney at the east end of the valley in a series of lakes.

Today most of the population in the Ili River Valley is Kazak, but in the past dozens of ethnic groups have roamed the area. Certainly the rich resources of abundant water, large grassland areas and a mild climate in this dry region of Asia made the Ili Valley the ideal cradle for the largely nomadic Eurasian cultures.

Very early in Chinese history the importance of maintaining relations with the Wusun people of the far West was already evident. The Wusun were nomadic, as all people of the Asian steppes were, and in early Chinese documents the Wusun capital was called Chigu. To strengthen political ties the Chinese sent a number of their princesses to Wusun leaders as brides. It must have

The Tekes Grassland lies along the Tekes He (River), which is one of the three major tributaries of the Ili River.

been a challenge for the young women of the Chinese nobility to adapt to a nomadic horseback life. It is said that the princesses thrived in their new home, and began the surprising habit of wearing pants, something no Chinese women would ever have done in the culture of Central China. This fashion was brought back to China by the princesses and caused great consternation. But in one form or another trousers for Chinese women were there to stay.

The Ili Valley was historically an area of invasion from the West. In 1762 the Qing Dynasty established the post of Ili River General to exercise military control over the large region both to the north and the south of the Tian Shan. The old headquarters for the military can still be visited today 5 miles (9 km) southeast of Huocheng. For over 150 years this far-flung military post was used by the Qing Dynasty until all administrative and military functions were moved to the northern city of Urumqi, outside the eastern end of the Ili Valley.

SAYRAM LAKE

Among the many jewels that lie hidden within the folds of the Tian Shan Range is the picturesque Sayram Hu (Lake). Nearly 200 sq. miles (500 sq. km) in size and situated on a high plateau, Sayram is the most beautiful lake in Xinjiang. It has been called the last teardrop of the Atlantic Ocean because it is believed that this is the furthest west warm, moist ocean air can reach. Spring and early summer around the lake are brilliant with fields of wild poppies, golden lilies and other alpine flowers. Thanks to its pleasant climate and abundant water supply the lake area makes an ideal pasture for breeding sheep, cattle and horses, of which there is a special Ili breed. The waters look even more brilliantly blue in early winter when set against the surrounding towering peaks covered with white snow.

Rich grasslands around the Sayram Lake is home to the Ili horses.

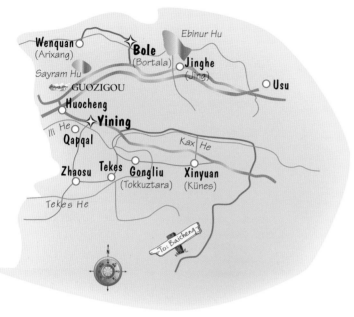

Guozigou

Guozigou (Fruit Valley) is an important pass through Tian Shan into the Ili Valley. A wide range of herbs and wild fruits including cherries, apples and apricots grow there. Genghis Khan is said to have first used the valley in his westward journeys, and the valley continued to be used by caravans traveling one of the Silk Routes characterized by trade in both directions. Today a modern road still uses Fruit Valley as the best route, giving travelers the opportunity to admire the color of the changing seasons in the valley's wildflowers and fruits.

A road winds through the Guozigou over Borohoro Shan, connecting the city Yining with northern Xinjiang.

Bayanbulak
and Other Scenic Regions in Tian Shan

In the northwestern provincial region of Xinjiang, China's second largest highland prairie of Bayanbulak is still home to wandering Mongolian herdsmen. The grasslands spread over 9,000 sq. miles (23,310 sq. km) at elevations that range from slightly under 5,000 ft. (1,530 m) to over 8,000 ft. (2,400 m). The luxurious grasslands are cool and humid in the summer and are supplied with abundant water from the region's rivers, lakes and swamps. Bayanbulak does justice to its Mongolian name that means rich fountains. Mongolians have long brought great herds of cattle, horses, sheep

The Bayanbulak Grasslands in their morning glory (opposite). They offer an ideal home for swans (above).

and camels to graze the endless grass in spring and summer. Summer visitors, amazed by the swaying green grass that covers the land to the horizon, may not realize that for half the year the grass is brown and lifeless. With the icy winds of winter on these open plains, the utility of the yurt, the traditional round nomadic dwelling made of draft-proof felt, is truly demonstrated.

Swan Lake

The abundant waters of Bayanbulak feed numerous springs and lakes. The best known is Swan Lake in the center of the Bayanbulak Grasslands. This large alpine lake is now one of the largest swan reserves in the

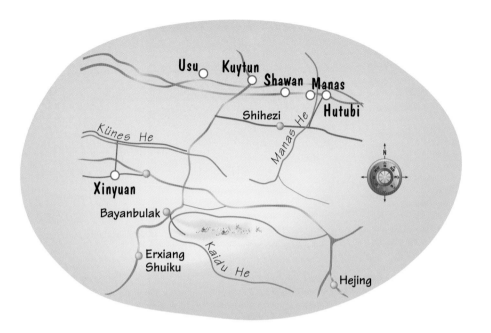

NALATI GRASSLANDS

From Bayanbulak a traveler can take a spectacular journey west through a pass in the Tian Shan (or Sky Mountains). The route follows a narrow gorge that is flanked by sheer cliffs. It is a pass that has been in long use by people of the area, but it is said the surprised soldiers of Genghis Khan's army named this beautiful expanse of green when they first beheld the high grassy valley spread before them. Nalati means sun-bathed slopes. At about 10,000 ft. (3,050 m) the grasslands of Nalati are a great contrast to the snowy Tian Shan, and a rare sight as they stretch to the snowy reaches of the mountains. This green, fertile valley at the eastern end of the Ili River Valley certainly deserves its nickname as the prairie in the sky.

GONGNAS VALLEY

About 60 miles (95 km) north of Bayanbulak, the green and lovely Gongnas Valley is home to a number of beautiful places to visit. The forested hillsides are an attraction in their own right. But there is also Fairy Lake, the Panchan Ravine, a remote Mongolian monastery and a group of highland hot springs. In the middle of this valley lies Gongnas River. It is often shrouded in mist and clouds. For half the year when the mist clears, the brilliant sunlight reveals the emerald green in its water, forests and grass. In winter a snowy blanket cloaks everything in pure white (see photo, pages 60–61).

world. Between spring and summer, tens of thousands of swans, some of them rare species, arrive to mate and breed. The swans share the lake with more than seventy other migrating species of birds as well as year-round waterfowl native to the area. As fall approaches, the migratory birds of Swan Lake begin their long flight back to southern China, India and as far away as southern Africa for the winter. Swan Lake is also the source of the Kaidu He (River) that flows into Bostan Lake, the largest freshwater lake in Xinjiang. The Chinese name for this river, Tongtian He, means river to heaven and is familiar to all who have read the Chinese classic, *Journey to the West*. Its winding path through the grasslands with a total of 1,142 bends and turns is unforgettable to those fortunate enough to have visited Bayanbulak.

Nalati Grasslands show a rich display of alpine flowers in the summer (opposite).

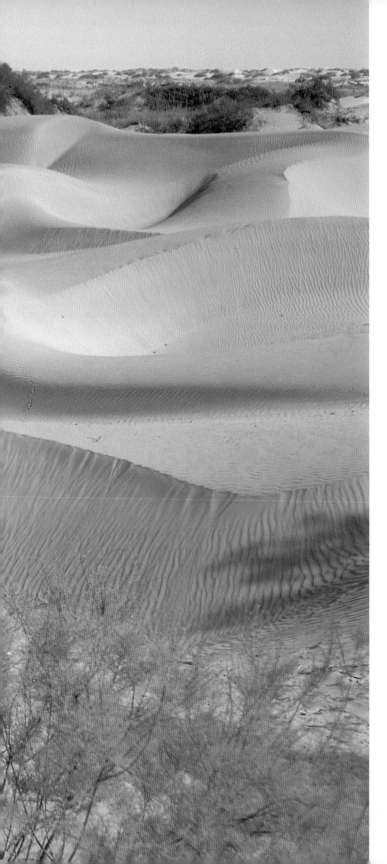

*K*orla,
the Kingdom of
Fragrant Pears

The vast northwestern provincial region of Xinjiang is mostly desert and endless grassy plains punctuated by tall mountain ranges. But in the south along the Silk Route there are a number of amazingly fertile oases. Water is the key, and delivery of the water from the surrounding mountains depends on an ancient but sophisticated system of irrigation called karez. This underground system requires great skill in building and maintaining, and it is said that the karez irrigation system was introduced several thousand years ago from Persia. Korla, lying on the southern slopes of Tian Shan (Sky Mountains), benefits from its geological layout. It is protected from the cold waves from the north by the mountain range, while the diversiform-leafed poplar forests along the Tarim River help to block the sandstorms from the south. Further nourished by the waters from the Kongque He (Peacock River), agriculture has been practiced here for more than two thousand years.

The Peacock River is fed by waters from Bostan Hu

Diversiform-leaf poplars can be found in the Korla region.

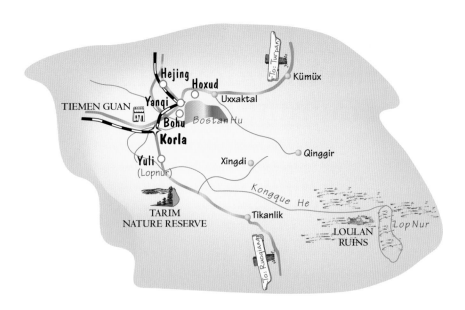

Local farmers sort a bountiful harvest of pears (above). The ancient Iron Gate Fortress (left below) used to guard the steep gorge.

(Lake), the biggest freshwater lake in Xinjiang, well stocked with a great variety of fish, such as the bighead, blunt-snout bream and crab. Its banks provide rich land for growing luxuriant and dense reeds and rushes. The upper reaches of the river has a 9-mile (14-km) -long gorge. It used to be the major passage into the Tarim Basin in ancient times, guarded by Tiemen Guan (Iron Gate Fortress), hence its name—Iron Fortress Gorge. Nowadays it is often referred to as the Haman Valley. About 3 miles (5 km) south of the Iron Gate Fortress lies the Korla oasis, where the city of Korla was established in 1758. Cotton and mulberries, the food of the silkworm, are ancient crops and have been the basis for the production of textiles in the region. Rice, corn and wheat are also grown here. The variety of fruits cultivated here include grapes grown on arbors, raisins, melons, figs, pomegranates and walnuts, along with the most famous Korla Pear or fragrant pear, which thrives in the region's hot dry climate and loose sandy soil. The Korla Pear was brought to the region long ago from further east in China. It is important to remember that the Silk Route was often the conduit for a wealth of influences and goods brought to China from much further west. From China came highly prized silk textiles that were unknown in the West and became a favorite with the Romans. But the eastward direction of traders on the Silk Route also brought much to China, and the rich agriculture of the region was greatly enhanced by these influences.

In the desert, oasis ponds provide precious water for human habitation and farming.

Stone City
on the Silk Road

In an open valley just east of the Pamir Plateau, which is known as the roof of the world, lies a quiet little town called Tashkurgan (or Taxkorgan). With only a couple of white-tiled hotels, a handful of restaurants, and a farmers' market, the town today is not very impressive. You can walk all its streets in less than an hour. Yet, this remote 13,100-ft. (4,000-m) high hamlet at the far western tip of China used to be a center of East-West communication and trade, and a stepping-stone to Persia and India on the Silk Road (or Route). Marco Polo stayed in Tashkurgan on his way to the court of Kubla Khan.

Tashkurgan is still the gateway from China to Tajikistan, Pakistan and Afghanistan. For many travelers, it is also a fabulous destination in itself. You can experience a way of life that doesn't seem to have changed very much since Marco Polo described it in the thirteenth century, breathe the unpolluted air of the high plateau, and view "the father of glaciers," 24,758-ft. (7,546-m) Mushitage Shan (Muztagh-Ata). The distant

The snowcapped mountains in the Pamir Plateau.

K2 (or Mount Qogir), the second tallest peak in the world at 28,251 ft. (8,611 m), can be seen towering in the far south in Pakistan. If you are very adventurous, you can take a trip with stunning mountain views between Tashkurgan and Kashgar (or Kashi) on the Karakoran Highway.

Tashkurgan has a population of 20,000. Eighty-five percent are Tajik, believed to be descendants of the ancient Aryans, who speak a form of Persian. The Tashkurganians believe they are the descendants of a Han (Chinese) princess and the sun, as recorded by the Tang Dynasty monk, Tripitaka, on his way back from his pilgrimage to India in search of Buddhist scriptures. In his writings on local customs, religious beliefs, and folklore, Tripitaka tells the story about a Han princess who was stranded by warfare on her way to Persia to be married to the king. To keep her safe, the special wedding envoy hid her in the mountains. Several months later, he discovered her pregnant, allegedly by the sun god. Afraid to deliver the bride in such a state, the envoy built a castle in the mountains and later enthroned the princess' son as the king. The remains of the legendary Princess Castle are perched on one of the steep mountain peaks about 50 miles (80 km) south of Tashkurgan.

Tashkurgan was the capital of the State of Puli two thousand years ago. Its name means "stone city or fort" in Turkic. At the end of the Tashkurgan valley there are still the remains of an ancient fort believed to have been built in the thirteenth century. Local houses, which are square and flat-roofed, are constructed of clay and

The interior of a Tajik yurt has an opening for ventilation and light.

stone in much the same manner as the ancient fort, though yurts are used when herds are moved from one pastureland to another. Another popular use of the stones is to deliver messages. If an item is found on the road, for example, the finder will put it by the side of the road and mark it with a stone.

Most Tajik people still live a half nomadic, half agricultural life. In spring, they plant cold-resistant crops, such as highland barley, wheat and peas, and then

move with their herds to better pasturelands. They return in the fall for harvesting. The Tajik like to say that they enjoy the freedom of the eagles. A popular Tajik proverb is "live like an eagle or die," and a totem pole of a flying eagle stands at the center of Tashkurgan.

The Tajik people are skillful riders. Snatching the sheep is a popular game (above). Though in ruins now, the dramatic Princess Castle (right) was believed to be built for a Han princess.

The *T*aklimakan Desert

In the local Uyghur language, Taklimakan means literally "a place you won't be able to get out of once you get in." Sitting in the center of the Tarim Basin in southern Xinjiang Uyghur Autonomous Region, the Taklimakan Desert is surrounded by three mountain ranges—Tian Shan in the North, Kunlun Shan and Altun Shan to the South. It stretches 620 miles (1,000 km) from Lop Nur in the East to the Kashi Oasis in the West and covers a vast area of more than 130,000 sq. miles (337,600 sq. km). It is the largest desert in China and the seventh largest in the world.

Although it has been crossed several times from South to North and even from West to East in the last few decades, the merchants and travelers who followed the Silk Road took great pains to avoid it. The desert is ringed by oases that have drawn farmers and herdsmen to its edges. Most of them are the Uyghur, people who live a simple but self-sufficient life raising sheep, cows, horses and camels, and growing melons, wheat and cotton. Yawantongguz Village is one such oasis that sits

about 62 miles (100 km) into the desert. Before the desert highway (opposite) was completed in 1995, it took three days of trekking or riding a camel to get to this village from any place in the area.

Sadly, the Taklimakan Desert continues to expand in a process called desertification. Drought and strong winds plus the continuing incursions of people and grazing animals are taking their toll on a delicately balanced environment. The Taklimakan Desert has moved

The oasis pond provides farming and drinking water for the villagers.

been appropriately called the "death sea of China."

The surface of the Taklimakan is composed of alluvial deposits several hundred feet thick and a cover of wind-blown sand about 1,000 ft. (300 m) thick. Complex wind conditions have created a variety of strangely shaped sand dunes from pyramids to arches to fish scales. More than 85 percent of the dunes are moving sand dunes. The most spectacular are two distinctively red and white sand dunes called the Holy Tomb Mount. Thanks to persistent wind erosion over the years, the top of the dune looks like a gigantic mushroom a dozen feet high that can shelter more than ten people under its umbrella.

The arc-shaped Mazartagh Mountain stretches some 62 miles (100 km) eastward and end at the Hotan He (River), well inside the desert. Erosion has carved the sandstone rock of these mountains into a series of "Buddhist shrines," which explains why the mountains were called Tongshen (Holy) Mountains in ancient times. A pass in the mountains served as a checkpoint on the Silk Road. Archaeological excavations at the pass have uncovered wooden scrolls written in ancient languages,

dozens of miles southward during the past thousand years. Scientists fear the rate is growing even faster.

Recent research confirms that the desert was formed some 4.5 million years ago while the Qinghai-Tibetan plateau was being raised, causing sand to rush into the basin.

Cut off from the sea by distance and mountains, the Taklimakan Desert has a typical continental climate. It is windy in the spring, scorching hot in the summer, and freezing cold in the winter. This desolate terrain has

The Loulan Ruins lies in Lop Nur to the east of the Taklimakan.

coins, wooden combs, iron arrows and other relics from the Tang Dynasty (AD 618–907). The ruins of Mazartagh Fort, dating from the eighth century or thereabouts, still stand on a slope of the Mazartagh Mountain. The site is a wonderful place to view the desolate beauty of the desert with its glistening sands and crescent sand dunes.

More than forty ancient city ruins have been discovered in Taklimakan Desert, principally on its southern edge, where oases encouraged the building of cities. Cities of the thirty-six Western Kingdoms, such as Niya, Yotkan and Loulan, were built there more than 2,000 years ago. While most of the ancient cities are ruins or have simply been buried by sand, a few sites have been worked on by archaeologists. At a Niya site, for example, excavators found printed floral fabrics and embroideries from the Eastern Han Dynasty (AD 25–220).

On the southern rim of the Taklimakan, seasonal rivers flow into the desert. The largest is the 500-mile (800-km) Hotan River that runs across the desert from south to north. Broad and shallow, the river is flanked by reeds, poplars and other kinds of drought-resistant trees and shrubs. With its vegetation, the river provides a green corridor in the desert that attracts some fifty kinds of animals.

A virgin forest of 77,400 acres (31,300 hectares) of diversiform-leaf poplars, as well as willows, shazao (the local date trees) and grass follow the Hotan River into the desert. These particular poplars (opposite) are considered living plant fossils with a history of more than 135 million years. Their leaves change to a brilliant gold in the late fall, transforming the look of the land.

Qinghai Hu, a Paradise for Birds

Qinghai is a large province on the Tibetan Plateau northeast of Tibet. Although it is one of China's most desolate areas, it is the source of the country's mightiest rivers–the Yellow River (Huang He), the Yangtze and the Lancang (or Mekong). The two major attractions for tourists who visit Qinghai are Ta'er Monastery, one of the six great Tibetan Yellow Hat Sect lamasteries and birthplace of the sect's founder, Tsongkhapa, and Qinghai Hu, China's largest saltwater lake.

Qinghai Hu is surrounded by three mountain ranges: the Sun Moon, the Datong and the Nan ranges that are about 93 miles (150 km) from Xining, Qinghai's capital city. The lake is also called Koko Nor (Dark Blue Lake) in Mongolian, and it justly deserves the name. Almost the size of the Great Salt Lake in Utah, Qinghai Hu is a spectacular sight framed by the surrounding grasslands and mountains. Its marshes that provide sheltered breeding territory, abundant fish and protected islands attract more than 100,000 birds every spring to breed and spend the summer. Some birds fly over the Himalayas to reach Qinghai Hu. In early fall the birds begin to migrate south before the cold weather comes.

There were once five distinct islands in the lake, Haixin Shan (Lake Center Hill), Sha Dao (Sand Island), Sankuaishi (Three Stones), Haixi Shan (West Lake Hill) and Haixi Pi (West Lake Shoal). Haixi Shan and Haixi Pi

On the way to Qinghai Hu (opposite), it's worth taking a side trip to the Ta'er Monastery (left) in Huangchuan.

The foot of the Sun Moon Mountain is covered by vast expanse of yellow rape flowers (above, left). Daotang He (Reverse Flow River) is a small river to the east of Qinghai Hu. Unlike other rivers in the region, it flows from east to west and feeds into the lake (above, right).

are often called the Bird Islands because they were once the principal bird breeding grounds. Continuing drought and expanding agriculture in the province have taken their toll on Qinghai Hu. (Farms near the lake were closed by the government in 2003.) As recently as the 1960s, 108 rivers fed into the lake; today only sixteen do. The water level of the lake has been dropping steadily by 4–6 in. (10–15 cm) annually for thirty years or more. One result is that many of the islands are now more aptly called peninsulas. Another result is increased salinity of the water, which has affected the population of the lake's single fish, the slow-growing huangyu, or scaly carp. Fishing is no longer allowed.

In spite of these changes, Qinghai Hu is still a paradise for birds. Wild geese, egrets, gulls, cormorants, sandpipers and very rare black-necked cranes are among the many varieties of birds that return each year. Between April and early July, you can see birds everywhere in the sky, beside the water and on their nests. Birds build their nests very close to one another at Qinghai Hu. Observers have counted as many as twenty-two nests in an area of 43 sq. ft. (4 sq. m). At times Haixi Shan is covered by so many bird eggs that it is known as Egg Island, while Haixi Pi is similarly referred to as Cormorant Island, since the cormorants nest there exclusively.

Today birds nest on all the islands. Sankuaishi has the biggest bird population, while the cliffs and shoals of Haixin Shan, the island in the middle of the lake, is a close second. This island, 0.6 mile (1 km) long and 253 ft. (77 m) high is reputed to be the birth place of a special breed of horse during the Tuyuhun era (329 – 663), the first empire of the Qinghai Plateau. During the Han Dynasty (206 BC to AD 220), it housed a monastery. Monks traveled to the island on foot in the winter when the lake was frozen, carrying with them supplies to last an entire year. They stayed until the next winter when they were able to walk back to the shore.

Among the principal residents of the Bird Islands are wild spotted-head geese with two black streaks on their heads. At the end of March, when the ice on the lake has not yet begun to melt, flocks of these geese arrive in their usual orderly way, flying in a straight line or a vee formation. They feed on grass and insects and are monogamous. Generally peaceful, they will fight as a group when any of their number are attacked.

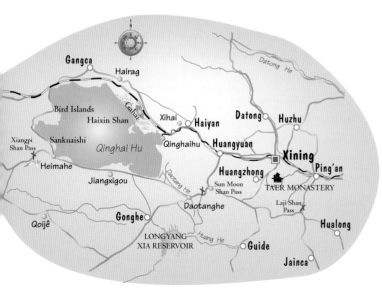

Birds fly to Qinghai Hu to feed and breed every year.

*S*ister Lakes
near the Source of the Yellow River

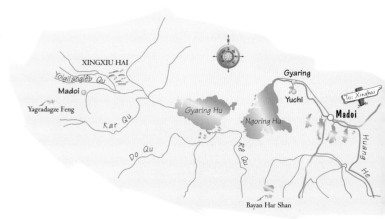

Situated at the heart of the Qinghai-Tibetan Plateau are two brilliant, clear freshwater lakes that lie no more than 12 miles (20 km) apart. Their Tibetan names are Gyaring, meaning silver white and Ngoring, meaning verdant blue. At over 13,780 ft. (4,200 m) high, the two sister lakes are connected by a small river, and together they were long considered the source of China's second longest river, the Huang He, or Yellow River.

While much of Qinghai is covered with desertlike terrain, the region around the Sister Lakes has been known for its generous natural resources since ancient times. As far back as the Han era (206 BC to AD 220), the native Qiang peoplee had already settled here, raising cattle, sheep and yaks. Horses bred here were prized throughout China. In the Tang Dynasty (618 to 907), the region became an important pathway between the South and North, especially with the increased trade between Central China and Tibet.

It is said that it was on the shores of Gyaring Lake in 641 that the Tibetan king, Songtsen Gampo, pitched a tent to welcome his bride, the Tang Princess Wencheng, before the couple traveled upstream along the Huang He

The lake shores of Gyaring are fertile grazing land for sheep and yaks.

over the Bayan Har Shan (Mountains) and on to Tibet.

It was only in the late twentieth century that the true headwaters of the Yellow River were traced to Kar Qu and Yoigilanglêb Qu, which originate to the west in a large oval basin in the northern foothills of the Bayan Har Mountains. The basin was once dotted with more than 100 ponds that fed a large year-round spring. From this spring the water flowed to a creek that ran into Gyaring Lake. So begins the famous Yellow River, that is the cradle of Chinese civilization. Recent droughts have dried up many of the ponds and water levels in the Sister Lakes have suffered as well. But these serene and beautiful lakes are still the source of the Yellow River, often called the River of Sorrows because of the devastation it has caused in China on its route to the sea.

Downstream from the Ngoring Lake, the Yellow River flows west through grasslands along a mountain, Anye Maqen, meaning "benevolent ancestor" (anye) and "the biggest mountain at the origin of the Yellow River" (maqen) in Tibetan. Anye Maqen is one of the four sacred mountains worshipped by the local Tibetans and believed to be the embodiment of one of the Tibetan gods. In the Tibetan year of the goat, pilgrims will make a week-long religious circuit, called a kora, around the mountain. Its main peak, Machen Gangri, shrouded by clouds most of the year, was once considered to be the highest peak in the world. A Chinese team scaled it in 1960 and found that although its towering 20,611-ft. (6,282-m) height is impressive, it is short of Mount Everest's height by 8,412 ft. (1,564 m).

An aerial view of Ngoring Lake.

The Chang Tang
Grasslands

ounded by the Nyainqêntanglha, Gangdisi and Kunlun mountains, the northern Tibetan Plateau (known as Chang Tang in Tibetan) is a high, cold, dry steppe as large as the part of the United States that is east of the Mississippi River. Chang Tang occupies half of the area of Tibet. With an average elevation of over 14,700 ft. (4,500 m), the northern Tibetan Plateau is indeed the roof of the world. A natural pastureland, the windswept plateau once supported a small population of hearty nomads and their yaks. New settlers and poachers have converged on the area, and their presence now threatens both man and beast. In 1993 the Chinese government, with the help of the Wildlife Conservation Society, created the Chang Tang Nature Reserve in the southwestern part of the plateau. Covering an area of 108,108 sq. miles (280,000 sq. km), it is the second largest nature reserve in the world.

Fifty years ago the land now in the reserve was rich in wildlife and virtually uninhabited. Today 25,000 nomads wander the region with their sheep and goats.

Lone horse grazing on the Chang Tang grasslands.

Similar inroads have been made on the rest of the northern Tibetan Plateau. The real threat, however, comes not from the growing population but from commercial hunters with four-wheel-drive vehicles and automatic weapons who have a ready market for the rare animals such as the Tibetan antelope, or chiru that live in the reserve. Chiru wool fetches high prices in Tibet and even higher prices in India where it is woven into scarves called shahtooshes. These scarves have been sold illegally all over the world for as much as $15,000 each. Other endangered species on the northern Tibetan Plateau include Tibetan gazelles, wild asses (kiangs), wild yaks, Tibetan argali sheep, snow leopards, Tibetan brown bears, wolves and lynx.

NAMTSO

There are at least thirty-five lakes that have an area of over 39 sq. miles (100 sq. km) on the northern Tibetan Plateau. By far the largest is Namtso, or Heavenly Lake. Surrounded by snowcapped peaks, Namtso is the highest saltwater lake in the world at 15,000 ft. (4,700 m) above sea level. Its surface is a bright sapphire blue and reflects the surrounding flowers in summer like a mirror. It is one of the four holiest lakes in Tibet and is regularly visited by thousands of Buddhist pilgrims from Tibet and elsewhere. Pilgrims perform the required circuit of the lake and worship at the four monasteries sited on each side of the lake. Five small islands in the lake are believed to be an incarnation of the Buddha of the Five

Prayer flags are dwarfed by the vastness of Namtso, the highest saltwater lake in the world (opposite).

Directions and are part of the attraction for pilgrims who have often made the long and difficult trip to the lake on foot. The five islands are covered with oddly shaped stones.

Not far from the Namtso is the town of Nagqu (or Nagchu), a regional business and cultural center on the Qinghai-Tibetan Highway. Every August thousands of herdsmen from all over the northern Tibetan Plateau ride into town for the Nagqu Horserace Festival. Almost overnight the visitors set up a white tent city near the town. Events continue for several days and include horse races, yak races, horsemanship displays, archery contests on horseback, horse trading, barter and performances by itinerant balladeers and dancers, as well as eating, drinking and catching up with old friends.

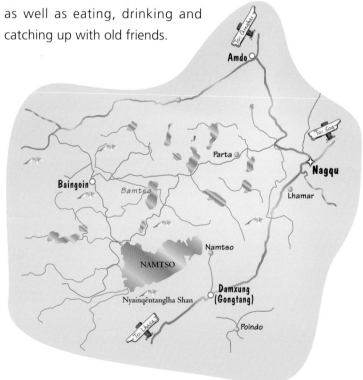

Exploring *Ngari* and Western Tibet

Kangrinboqê Feng (or Mount Kailash) in western Tibet is considered to be the most sacred mountain by the Tibetan Buddhists in a land of holy mountains. Believers in Bön, Tibet's ancient nature worship, Hindus and Jains from India also venerate this lovely snow-capped peak. To the Tibetan Buddhists it is the earthly manifestation of the heavenly home of the gods, high on the list for all Tibetan pilgrims to visit. Pilgrims who perform one hundred and eight circuits, called koras, around Kangrinboqê believe they can attain Buddhahood and forego the endless cycle of death and rebirth, but all pilgrims make at least one kora. Sometimes a pilgrim performs the kora as a grueling series of repeated prostrations around the mountain, a journey that takes walkers at least a day. The Tibetan name means Precious Jewel of Snow, which is a fitting description of this snowy pinnacle that rises from a desolate plain framed by brilliant blue sky.

Mount Namo Nanyi, or Gurla Mandhata towers at 25,356 ft. (7,728 m) to the north of Mapam Yumtso (opposite). The holy Kangrinboqê Feng is lit by a rosy sunset glow (right).

Before Western explorers were allowed to enter Tibet, the Kangrinboqê region was believed to be the source of several of the great rivers in Asia. It was not until modern times that the four rivers springing from the Kangrinboqê region were traced and identified as the rivers Tibetans have associated with the four cardinal directions: the Sênggê Zangbo that becomes the Indus, Langqên Zangbo or the Sutlej, Damqog Zangbo, the origin of the Yarlung Zangbo that in India is called the Brahmaputra, and Mmabja Zangbo that becomes in India the Karnali, a tributary of the Ganges.

During a period in Tibetan history, the conflicts between adherents to the newer faith of Buddhism and the older Bön beliefs resulted in the defeat of Buddhists and removal of the Buddhist faith in large parts of Tibet. Small areas, often isolated from each other, continued the Buddhist tradition with the Guge Kingdom in western Tibet providing a refuge for the faith. The capital of

A wall mural at Tsaparang depicting the life of the Guge Kingdom is still in brilliant colors (below), while the ruins of Tsaparang (opposite) are a fascinating maze of clay at the foot of craggy hills.

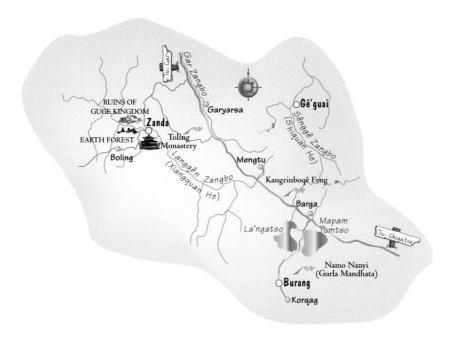

the Guge Kingdom was Tsaparang. The ruins of this once powerful tenth-century kingdom are the remains of extensive buildings, tunnels and cave dwellings made of clay. Some of the murals that depict the life of this once thriving place are still visible. Temples, residences, defensive structures and hidden escape tunnels attest to the genius of the builders.

MAPAM YUMTSO

Mapam Yumtso (or Lake Manasarovar), meaning "Unsurpassed Lake" in Tibetan, lies close to the sacred Kangrinboqê Feng in southwestern Tibet near the border with Nepal. It is one of the holy lakes in Tibet. According to some Tibetan records, the lake is actually the Yaochi, or Emerald Pond, where the Chinese Heavenly Mother of the West resides.

THE EARTH FOREST IN ZANDA

The earth forest in Zanda (or Zhanda) with its sand-rock formations of caves, stone trees and canyons is a unique landscape, shaped as a result of gradual geological movements and the erosion caused by wind and water. It covers an area of over 77 sq. miles (200 sq. km) on the river banks of the Langqên Zangbo (or Xiangquan He), near the ruins of the Guge Kingdom.

Mapam Yumtso (left) is situated near Tibet's border with Nepal. The work of erosion leaves a bizarre stone forest in Zanda (opposite).

Shigatse
and the Tashilhunpo Monastery

The second largest town in Tibet, Shigatse, at the junction of the Yarlung Zangbo and Nyang-chu rivers, was once the capital of the Tibetan province of Tsang and held the greatest political power during the sixteenth century. Meaning "fertile land" in Tibetan, Shigatse is known for its grand Tashilhunpo Monastery, the traditional seat of the Panchen Lamas, and for the ruins of the king's castle, or dzong, which is on the route pilgrims take as they circle the monastery.

A visit to the huge Tashilhunpo Monastery is an opportunity to see a city within a city that was built to house thousands of monks. In addition to a great number of temples and tombs, the monastery has a Philosophy College, a Tantric College, living quarters, an assembly hall, a vast kitchen and dining hall and offices to oversee the running of such a large institution. Pilgrims have a prescribed route within the monastery—through temples and past a wall nine stories high used to unfurl tankas, elaborately painted cloth pictures of the Buddha, during the summer festivals. The circuit

A blanket of spring wildflowers in Shigatse (opposite) and a glimpse of Tashilhunpo Monastery through one of its gates (right).

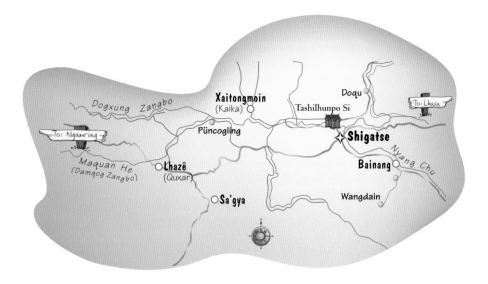

begins at the Maitreya Temple that houses a giant seated Buddha covered in gold. A circuit is taken around the giant statue of Maitreya who is the Buddha of the Future, or Champa in Tibetan. The seated Buddha is nearly 9 ft. (2.5 m) tall. On his lotus throne the Buddha's right thumb and forefinger touch in a circle that symbolizes teaching. This gesture is just one of several symbolic gestures familiar to all Buddhists. Tibetans believe the Buddha of the future will return only when all humans have achieved deliverance from suffering. The stream of visitors continues down a passage lined with tiny chapels and passes through several tombs of Panchen Lamas who have made Tashilhunpo their home. Some of the monastery buildings are quite recent, but the pilgrim circuit also passes through the oldest parts of the monastery where monks engage in religious debate in the courtyard of the Philosophy College.

Inside the great monastery complex.

Shannan, the Cradle of Tibetan Civilization

The spectacular landscape of the Yarlung Zangbo Valley of southern Tibet is rich in history, and it is also Tibet's most important agricultural area. The Yarlung Zangbo (River) flows from west to east along this valley, called Shannan in Tibetan, and it is here at elevations of 10,000–13,000 ft. (3,000–4,000 m) that most of the grain and other crops cultivated in Tibet are grown. Tibetans venerate what they have identified as the first cultivated ground in this valley, and local farmers still bring back to their fields a bit of the soil from what is said to be the very first field in Tibet to promote a good harvest. Their offspring eventually found that wild plants alone did not provide enough food for the growing population. Thankfully, heavenly gods interceded by sowing the very first seeds of wheat and rye near the Monkey Caves. The monkey people learned to cultivate this first food crop and forever after cherished the soil of this first piece of cultivated land just to the northwest of the Monkey Caves of Gangpo Ri in the area of Tsetang.

The Yamzho Yumtso looks like a giant piece of sapphire.

On the hill near Tsetang stand the ruins of the Yumbulagang Palace (above), said to be the earliest palace in Tibet, built in the second century for King Nyentri Tsenpo. Legend holds that a herdsman tending his livestock spotted a small child on a mountaintop. The herdsman thought the child must be a cherub from heaven. He carried the child home on his shoulders. Later the child became the first ruler of the early Tubo Kingdom whose capital was in the Yarlung Valley. One of the surviving portions of the palace is a tower that houses statues of Buddha, ancient rulers of Tibet and two foreign princesses, the Princess Wencheng of China and Princess Bhrikut of Nepal, brought to Tibet for the purpose of political alliance through marriage.

South of Tsetang traces of the burial mounds of the Tubo kings can be found. The harsh Tibetan climate has made it difficult to identify all of these tombs from the seventh to eighth centuries. According to historical records there should be thirteen burial sites, and only nine have been located. Three are identified as belonging to Songtsen Gampo who moved the Tibetan capital to Lhasa; King Tride Songsten marked by an elegantly carved stele, and Trisong Detsen whose tomb is guarded by a pair of stone lions.

Gradually the Tibetan form of nature worship called Bön was replaced by Buddhism brought in from India in the third century. Samye Monastery, one of the oldest in Tibet on the north side of the Yarlung Zangbo, is where the Great Debate, the famous religious showdown lasting several years in the late eighth century, took place.

This famous early monastery was built in the shape of a mandala, a round symbol sacred in Tibetan Buddhism. The buildings of the Samye Monastery symbolize the universe as a central building surrounded by two concentric circles, one of four temples, the other of eight temples forming the outer ring of the mandala. The monastery was built in AD 779, only after the site was consecrated and cleared of wrathful demons by the famous Guru Rinpoche. Trisong Detsen, the Tibetan king at that time, bolstered the plan for the construction of one of the first monasteries in Tibet. Although Samye Monastery has been rebuilt several times, the obelisk still stands in the monastery carved with a proclamation that Buddhism was the religion of Tibet, and exhorting all Tibetans to follow Buddhist teachings and to support the monastery.

The burial mound of Songtsen Gampo is one of the three identified.

The layout of the Samye Monastery (opposite) was designed to represent the ideal universe described in Buddhist scriptures. Tibetan pilgrims perform kora around sacred mountains (above).

Another monastery near the Yarlung Zangbo is the famous Tradrug Monastery. A dramatic tale of its construction involves a bottomless lake inhabited by a five-headed dragon. A famous handler of hunting hawks was invited to do battle with this terrible beast. After a seven-day struggle the dragon was subdued and the deep water subsided. But the founder of the monastery, Songtsen Gampo, took no chances. He filled the lake with all his treasures as the foundation and named the monastery "the hawk that roars like a dragon."

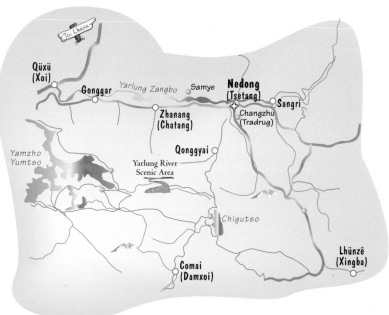

The **Yarlung Zangbo**
Gorge

The great Yarlung Zangbo (River) has its source in the eternally snowcapped peaks on the north side of the highest mountain range in the world, the Himalayas. The Yarlung Zangbo first sweeps down to the Tibetan Plateau to its namesake valley and continues its journey eastward in Tibet through the broad Yarlung Zangbo Valley where the greatest population of Tibet lives. This river valley, the highest in the world, is the product of great tectonic plate movement more than fifty million years ago. As the Indian Plate moved north and collided with the Eurasian Plate, the Himalayan Range rose from what was once a seabed and the Yarlung Zangpo Valley was created at the juncture of the two plates. Near Lhasa the riverbed of the Yarlung Zangbo has yielded grains of sedimentary rock that contain a record of the alternating patterns of earth's magnetic field. The river winds its way east through Tibet, but suddenly makes a hairpin turn coursing south into India where it is known as the famous Bramhaputra

The Yarlung Zangbo cuts a deep gorge (right) through snowcapped mountains. It makes a U-turn at Mount Namche Barwa (opposite).

River that eventually empties in the Bay of Bengal. Outstanding topographical features of the Yarlung Zangbo region include glaciated peaks, dramatic gorges and limestone deposits characterized by sinks, ravines and underground streams.

The rain shadow on the north side of the Himalayas means that there is very little rainfall in most of the Yarlung Zangbo Valley, but at the lower elevations crops such as barley, buckwheat and potatoes are grown and animals graze. Although the entire length of this Himalayan river valley is fascinating, the part of the river that has gained special attention is where it turns south and enters the deepest and longest river gorge in the world. At one point in its descent the Yarlung Zangbo plunges through a narrow gorge 16,000 ft. (4,800 m) deep, three times as deep as the Grand Canyon. Along the length of the Yarlung Zangbo there are a variety of habitats at different elevations. After leaving the highest snowy elevation at the river's source, there is a long, gentle descent from the river valley habitat that is really a cold desert. Next comes a steppe environment and then deciduous scrub and grasses. At a much lower elevation of around 10,000 ft. (3,000 m), the vegetation changes to conifer forests with rhododendrons, which are native to the area.

In the valley of the lower Yarlung Tsangpo River lies the remote town of Medog (Motuo). It is cut off from the rest of the world six months out of a year. When it is accessible, one has to cross through snowcapped mountains in trucks and hike for two or three days through

An avalanche on Mount Namche Barwa tumbles into the gorge.

Precarious paths hug the cliffs of the deep gorge.

forests, muddy swamps and streams to get there. Though surrounded by towering mountains, such as the Namche Barwa at 25,447 ft. (7,756 m) and Gyala Baidie Peak at 22,967 ft. (7,284 m) above sea level, Medog has a surprisingly low altitude, averaging at about 3,900 ft. (1,200 m), which is a sub-tropical and humid zone with breathtaking scenery. Because of its inaccessibility, Medog is known as a paradise for animals, home to thousands of insects and forty-two protected animals, including the Bengal tigers.

The Central Region

Bashang
and a Side Trip to Shangdu

Between the low plains of Hebei Province and the high Inner Mongolia Plateau, the land rises like a giant step in a staircase. This area is known as the Bashang Plateau (Bashang means "on top of the plain" in Chinese), a 6,178 sq. mile (16,000 sq. km) mixture of forests, marshes and grasslands that cover low rolling hills. Rivers, lakes and ponds keep the Bashang Plateau healthy and green. It has become a favorite destination for nature lovers and people who enjoy outdoor recreation, such as hiking, bicycling and camping.

One of the most beautiful grasslands in China, the Bashang Plateau offers year-round visual pleasure. Spring brings lush green grass; summer offers bursts of color with the blooming of wildflowers; fall shows off golden birch leaves and grass against a colorful background of red and orange shrubbery; and winter offers snow-laden trees in a pristine white world. From spring

The Bashang Plateau is a mixture of forests, marshes and grasslands, perfect for animal husbandry.

Autumn color in the birch forests in Saihanba National Forest Park (opposite).

through fall the plateau's undulating hills are covered with grasses of varying shades of green and gold cut through by zigzagging streams and an occasional cluster of sheep or cattle. The Bashang Plateau ranges from 4,820 to 6,900 ft. (1,500 to 2,100 m) above sea level.

Beautiful sites are scattered all over the area, such as Saihanba National Forest Park, Birch Forest Valley, Qicai (Seven Colored) Gorge, Lama Shan, Jiangjun Paozi (General's Lake) and many others. The most popular and easiest to reach is the Mulan Weichang (Hunting Ground) in Weichang County at the eastern end of the plateau. It was established in 1681, the twentieth year of Emperor Kangxi's reign, for royal hunts every fall with his military. Covering an area of over 4,000 sq. miles (10,450 sq. km) of different terrain, there were more than 100 royal hunts during a period of 140 years under the reigns of the emperors Kangxi, Qianlong and Jiaqing. Now, of course, royal hunts are a thing of the past, but stone stela and rock carvings inscribed in Manchu, Han, Mongol and Tibetan still record the details of these hunts.

Many historical events are linked to Mulan, most particularly the ancient Ulan Butong Battle in 1690. That year Gardan, lord of the Junger Tribe, staged rebellions against the central government that were quelled by repeated punitive expeditions. Emperor Kangxi personally led three of them and finally defeated Gardan. The Mongolian areas were reunified under the central Qing Dynasty. Tong Guogang, Kangxi's maternal uncle, died in one of the battles near a lake that was later

named General's Lake. It is a popular scenic spot in nearby Saihanba National Forest Park.

While in Bashang, an interesting side trip is to the ruins of Shangdu, the Yuan Dynasty capital, on the north bank of the Shandian He (or River) in Inner

The General's Lake in its pristine state.

corners. Inside the Forbidden City were Daming Hall, Kuizhang Pavilion and Da'an Pavilion. Government offices once stood on its neatly planned streets. The Outer City wall was built of earth. Inside were gardens, temples and workshops. The neighborhoods outside the city's east, south and west gates were comprised of markets, residences, and warehouses. The city fell in the early years of Ming Emperor Yongle's reign in the fourteenth century, but the walls and the foundations of buildings still stand as an invaluable research site for Yuan Dynasty history.

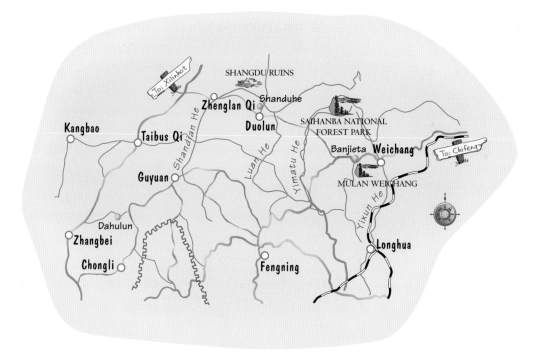

Mongolia. This square-shaped city was built in 1256 using a design typical of central China. The layout incorporated a Forbidden City, Imperial City and Outer City, all of which were constructed symmetrically along a central axis. The walls of the Forbidden City were covered with brick and watchtowers were built at the four

The pastoral country around Princess Lake (opposite). The ruins of Shangdu is in the middle of the grasslands north of Luan He (above).

The Magical World of the *Misty Spirit Mountain*

In the Yan Shan Range in the province of Hebei north of Beijing, there towers the Misty Spirit Mountain, famous around China for the mists that gather around it and the surrounding peaks. Admirers of atmospheric mist-shrouded landscapes have long roamed the area and climbed the Misty Spirit Mountain, or Wuling Shan in Chinese, to witness the sea of mist that wreathes the peaks and fills the valleys below. Early mornings are the ideal time to catch sight of the mountain peaks revealed above a swirling mist. These mountaintops have long been compared to tiny fishing boats adrift on an ocean of clouds or dragons at play, their misty breath curling around the peaks. For many visitors, the Misty Spirit Mountain is a magical place.

Visitors come to Misty Spirit Mountain for the mists and to escape the blistering heat of Beijing summers. At 6,983 ft. (2,116 m), the Misty Spirit Mountain is the tallest mountain in the region, and the welcome coolness can change to chilly temperatures, especially in the

Waitao (Odd-Shaped Peach) Peak is the summit of Yan Shan Range, with an elevation of 6,983 ft. (2,116 m).

Longtan (Dragon's Pond) Waterfall cascades in a deep ravine.

early morning and evening. In addition, the entire area is part of a large nature reserve set aside in 1984 to protect the disappearing temperate forest in this region of China. The reserve boasts the reclusive leopard as Wuling Shan's largest resident. The rhesus macaque, rare this far north in China, is also on the list of protected species. Wuling Shan is also a destination for bird

watchers who come to enjoy the great variety of birds such as the golden eagle, the long-eared owl and the brown-eared pheasant. The fact that in 1645 the area was declared forbidden to enter and was reserved for imperial tombs helped to keep this mountainous area near Beijing unspoiled.

Hikers on Misty Spirit Mountain pass through great stands of Dahurian larch, fir and mountain poplar. Wildflowers thrive in the cool environment and a type of bellflower is found only in this region of Hebei. A great variety of medicinal herbs grow on the mountain's slopes, including the highly prized ginseng. Man-made works add delight to a visit. Liu Bowen, a Ming Dynasty poet, left his apt description of Wuling Shan as "The Cool Terrain of the Misty Spirit Mountain" high on a

northern slope carved on an oval stone almost 100 ft. (30 m) high.

In the area of the mountain called Phoenix Peak, there are the ancient remains of several drinking wells that may have been the work of monks who, legend says, built a temple and dug seven wells in the rocks. There are also a number of unusual rock formations. One resembles a pagoda with a stream of water rippling at the foot and is called the Fairy Pagoda Gully. There is Lotus Pond that, when seen from above, mimics an open lotus, and Heavenly Peach Peak (Xiantao Peak), the name of the rock formation at the top of the mountain where two mammoth rocks lie like a pair of peaches at an angle. It is said that the mountain's many caverns form an underground palace of stalactites, stalagmites and stone columns. They remain unexplored and add to the mysterious beauty of the Misty Spirit Mountain.

A side trip is to the magnificent section of the Great Wall on Mount Jinshanling (opposite). Situated about 80 miles (130 km) northwest of Beijing, it is near the town of Bakeshiying in Hebei Province. To the east is the Misty Spirit Mountain, while due west is the Wohu Ling (or Crouching Tiger Ridge). The Jinshan-ling section of the wall is 12 miles (20 km) long and makes a wonderful scenic hike. It was built in 1567 under the leadership of two famous Ming Dynasty generals, Qi Jiguang and Tan Lun, who demanded superb workmanship on the wall and its many watchtowers. Restored for tourists only in recent years, the Jinshanling Great Wall has fewer visitors than other Great Wall sites but with equally impressive vistas.

Weishan Hu, a Lake of Treasures

Weishan Hu is the largest lake in the central China province of Shandong. An aerial view of the lake shows it is shaped like a giant silkworm. A freshwater lake, it covers some 455 sq. miles (1,180 sq. km).

According to ancient records, this part of Shandong Province used to be dotted with hundreds of tiny lakes, but they converged into a dozen larger lakes after the Yellow River twice flooded the area in the Han Dynasty (206 BC–AD 220). By the twelfth century, river silt blocked the outlet of the Sishui River and formed four connected lakes: Nanyang, Dushan, Zhaoyang and Weishan. All four lakes are often referred to collectively as Weishan Hu, which is the largest of the four.

China's Grand Canal, started 2,500 years ago, was once the longest man-made waterway in the world. Running 1,000 miles (1,610 km) from Hangzhou in the south to Beijing in the north, it was cut right through the lakes.

Dubbed "the treasure house," Weishan Hu boasts 78 species of fish, 74 water plants and 87 species of birds. Carp and tortoise from Weishan Hu were on the list of royal tributes brought to the emperor of the Qing Dynasty (1644–1911). The lake also has 16,500 acres (6,660 hectares) of lotus plants. In July and August

when the lotus flowers are in blossom, the area is completely covered with green lotus leaves and white and pink flowers. A lotus flower festival is held here every August to celebrate this breathtaking sight.

Weishan Dao Island, named after the Shang Dynasty Prince Weizi, sits in the center of Weishan Hu. Prince Weizi's 32-ft. (10-m) -high tomb sits atop a hill at the northwest end of the island. A small museum in the cemetery has Shang Dynasty (1766–1122 BC) and Han Dynasty (206 BC–AD 220) relics.

Boats still traffic between Weishan Hu's islands and along the Grand Canal (above).

In the summer, the lakes are covered by thousands of acres of green lotus leaves and pink flowers. Lotus seeds and roots are a major crop for the inhabitants around the lakes.

The Wild Hongyuan Grassland

In the far north of Sichuan Province, bordering Gansu Province in the North and Qinghai Province in the West, lies an expanse of Hongyuan Grassland on the banks of the Bai He, or White River. The largest of three grasslands on the Aba Plateau, the Hongyuan area is inhabited mostly by Tibetan herdsmen. In the river valley, herds of cattle and sheep graze the deep green grass under a canopy of blue sky, with scattered white yurts of the shepherds making a picturesque tableau.

The most beautiful spot on the Hongyuan Grassland is an area called Moon Estuary, where crescent-shaped inlets cut across the grassland, reflecting the blue sky and white clouds on sunny days. In the evening, the waterways zigzag through the grassland like a silver chain. Moon Estuary was once a vast marshland, but an irrigation system tapped the marshland's water and this water management effort has turned the swampy area into lush pasture.

Later, roads were built to connect the Hongyuan

Grassland to Nuoergai in the North, Maerkang in the South, Jiuzhaigou and Huanglong scenic areas in the East and the town of Aba in the West. With a subtropi-

The White River twists and turns through the Hongyuan grassland (opposite). Locals ride their specially decorated cattle at festivals.

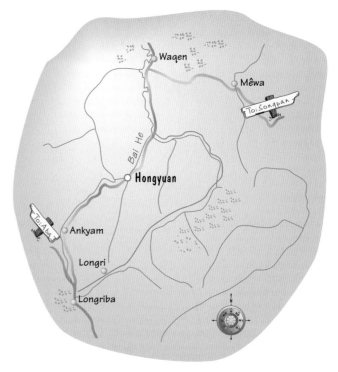

cal continental climate and an annual rainfall of 29 in. (728 mm), Hongyuan Grassland is ideal for raising rape-seeds, barley and various Chinese medicinal herbs.

To the north of Hongyuan Grassland lies the swampy area of the Songpan Grassland where the Bai He flows into the Yellow River. Only a tiny tributary of the Yellow River, the Bai He originates in the Aba Plateau and flows gently through the Hongyuan Grassland, irrigating the land and nurturing the livestock. Thanks to this small river, generations of Tibetans have been able to prosper.

The pilgrims pay their tribute to the monks (left) and then circumam-bulate the Mêwa Monastery (opposite).

THE DHARMA WHEEL MONASTERY

Commonly known as Mêwa Monastery for its location in Mêwa, Hongyuan County, the Dharma Wheel Monastery is a Longchen Rapjam monastery of the Nyingma School. It was originally built in 1646 in Garze County. In 1938 the monastery was moved to Mêwa. The current monastery was rebuilt in 1990 after its destruction in the late 1960s. It houses several hundred resident monks.

The Beauty of
Jiuzhaigou

Beautifully decorated houses stand out against green mountains.

The picturesque landscape of Jiuzhaigou (Nine Village Valley) has for centuries lain hidden and undisturbed by the outside world, cherished only by the Tibetan herdsmen and farmers who lived there. Now a nature preserve, Jiuzhaigou can be reached by intrepid visitors via a long bus ride or short flight from Chengdu, the provincial capital of Sichuan. The mountain-ringed valley boasts 108 alpine lakes. Many of these are what geologists call classic ribbon lakes in glacially formed valleys, dammed by avalanche rockfalls and stabilized and terraced by carbonate deposits.

But local Tibetans have a more romantic story about the origin of the lakes. They say the warrior god Dage once made a magic mirror. He gave it as a gift to the goddess Wunosemo, who accidentally dropped the mirror. The magic mirror shattered into 108 pieces, and each piece became an alpine lake.

Located in the northwest of Sichuan, Jiuzhaigou is made up of three valleys, Shuzheng, Rize and Zechawa, each 9 to 12 miles (14 to 18 km) long, that form the let-

Shuzheng Lakes (opposite) are framed by brilliant autumn colors.

ter Y. Jiuzhaigou originally contained nine Tibetan villages, as its name implies. Its attraction to visitors lies in its idyllic beauty. The sparkling lakes, tiered waterfalls and colorful tufa shoals combine to create a fairyland landscape. The 278-sq.-mile (720-sq.-km) valley can be covered in one day by tour bus, but a walking tour is the best way to enjoy the valley's unique natural wonders and to avoid the crowds. Once in the valley, well-marked boardwalks wind along mountain creeks, cut through forests and grasslands, cross lakes and waterfalls, and pass Tibetan villages.

The Lakes

The lakes of Jiuzhaigou range in color from emerald green to sapphire blue and all the variations in between. They even sound different: the deep lakes are quiet and subdued; those with shallow shoals bubble and sing; those with steep cliffs, dance and roar.

Of the 108 alpine lakes, the 5-mile (8-km) -long Changhai (Long Lake) at the end of Zechawa Valley is the longest and largest lake. With an elevation of over 10,000 ft. (3,100 m), the lake is surrounded by snow-capped peaks year round. Locals claim that a prehistoric monster (something similar to Scotland's Loch Ness monster) inhabits the lake. In fact, there seem to be no living things in the lake, not even fish.

The Wuhuahai (or Five Flower Lake) in the Rize Valley is one of the most spectacular, especially in late fall when reflections of colorful autumn leaves in the calcium-carbonate rich waters intermingle with the colors of underwater aquatic plants.

Another fascinating lake is the blue Wolonghai or Sleeping Dragon Lake. Under the surface of its water lies an ivory-colored calcareous tufa dike that looks like a sleeping dragon. It lies motionless when the water is tranquil and undisturbed, but seems to move when the lake surface is disturbed by wind.

Many lakes in Jiuzhaigou have fallen logs, some of which have calcified branches that float on the surface, becoming fertile ground for other plants (see photo, page 126).

Changhai (Long Lake) lies at the end of the Zechawa Valley.

THE WATERFALLS

Just as appealing as the lakes are waterfalls such as the Shuzheng Waterfalls at the top of a group of tiered lakes, the Panda Lake Waterfalls and the Pearl Shoal Waterfall (see photo, below), which is a 656-ft. (200-m) -wide fall over a shallow shoal with clusters of shrubs growing at the water's edge. But the most spectacular of all is the Nuorilang Waterfall (see photo, pages 130–131), which is a 886-ft. (270-m) -wide waterfall with a 79-ft. (24-m) drop at the juncture of the Shuzheng and Rize valleys. The name of the waterfall means "a male god" in Tibetan, which implies its magnificence and splendor. It does full justice to the power and beauty of the waterfall whose thunderous roar can be heard and felt through the forest long before it is seen.

THE ZARU MONASTERY

Close to the mouth of the valley on the Zaru Horse Trail, stands Zaru Si (Monastery). It is a typical lamasery with a main hall, Sutra Repository Tower, music stage, tearoom and guesthouse. It was first built in the seventeenth century, and has been renovated several times in its history, most recently in 2004. On the fifteenth of every third lunar month, the local Tibetans gather at the monastery to celebrate their Mazhi Festival with singing, dancing and chanting sutras for Buddhist worship.

The roof of the Zaru Monastery is decorated with a golden wheel and two deer. The symbols come from a legendary meeting between Buddha and his two students, the great gods, Brahma and Indra. According to the story, Buddha retired to an isolated place after he attained enlightenment. While sitting in meditation, he was approached by Brahma, holding a golden dharma wheel with a thousand spokes, and Indra, bearing a white, right-turning conch shell. They offered these objects to Buddha and requested the teachings on the holy dharma. Buddha said he would turn the wheel of

Stupas (chorten in Tibetan) are important religious monuments. Commonly called "white stupas," they house items that Buddhists hold sacred.

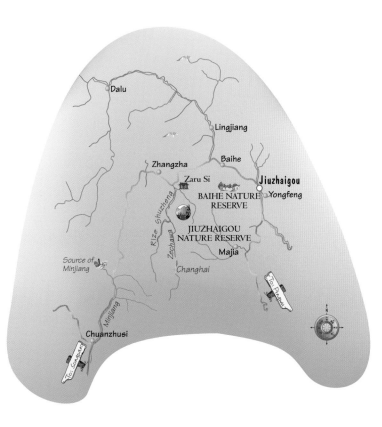

the dharma in three stages. Just then two deer emerged from the nearby forest and gazed directly at the wheel. To commemorate this first turning of the wheel, a dharma wheel and a pair of deer, male and female, sit on top of every Tibetan Buddhist temple and monastery. The wheel symbolizes the Buddha's teachings, and the deer represent his students, Brahma and Indra. The stance of the deer also carries significant meanings: their up-turned faces symbolize listening; their attentive gaze, reflection; and their reclining posture, meditation. Six golden metal gyaltsen (victory banners), symbolizing victory over negative forces from all directions, complete the roof decoration.

The recently renovated Zaru Monastery in Jiuzhaigou.

The Vistas of
Huanglong

Huanglong (Yellow Dragon) Scenic Area is about 35 miles (56 km) from the 2,500-year-old town of Songpan in northwest Sichuan Province. The area lies in a small valley, covered almost entirely by milky yellow calcium carbonate that looks like a long yellow dragon winding through dark green conifer forests. Colorful ponds (see photo, pages 136–137), waterfalls, gorges and snowcapped peaks add to the drama of the view. Although terraced ponds and eerie limestone topography are not rare in China, the scale, variety of colors and number of ponds at Huanglong make it a unique sight. About 2,300 ponds are scattered throughout the 2-mile (3.5-km) -long and 1,150-ft. (350-m) -wide valley that stands at an elevation of 10,000 ft. (3,200 m).

The scenic region starts at the Fuyuan Bridge. Not far from the bridge is a cluster of a dozen ponds called Guest Welcoming Ponds. Each pond has a different color, depending on the amount of organic and inorganic deposits caught by the pond's calcium dikes, which can be as small as a few inches or as tall as 7 ft. (2 m).

Natural terracing occurs on the mountain slope near Huanglong (opposite). Glistening Golden Sand Shoal snakes through the valley like a yellow dragon (right).

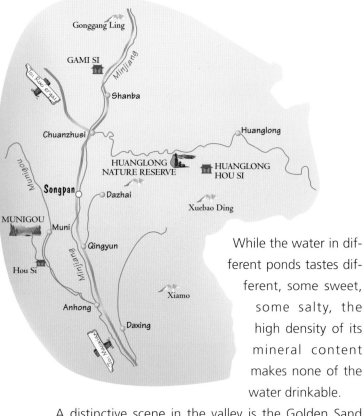

has about five hundred ponds of all shapes in distinct colors of blue, green and gold. The most spectacular group of ponds is at the end of the valley: Wucaichi (Multicolored Ponds). In the middle of its four hundred ponds are two stone pagodas built in the Ming Dynasty (1368–1644). Partly covered by travertine, these two pagodas guard the surrounding ponds and what is believed to be the tomb of the grandson of Cheng Yaojing, a famous Tang Dynasty general.

Huanglong Hou Si (Rear Temple), one of the three Taoist temples spaced at an equal distance of a mile from the other, is also worth visiting. While the front temple has disintegrated, the middle and rear temples are well preserved. Huanglong Hou Si is the most spectacular. It sits 11,674 ft. (3,558 m) above sea level,

While the water in different ponds tastes different, some sweet, some salty, the high density of its mineral content makes none of the water drinkable.

A distinctive scene in the valley is the Golden Sand Shoal, a 230- to 394-ft. (70- to 120-m) -wide strip of travertine that drops 4,920 ft. (1,500 m) from the forests. With sunlight reflecting off it, the travertine glistens like a yellow dragon coming to life. Down at the bottom of the shoal, there is a 23-ft. (7-m) drop where the water falls over the 131-ft. (40-m) -wide travertine wall with several caves called the Bathing Caves. Legend has it that the immortals used to bathe here. Women hope to be blessed with pregnancy after they bathe in these caves.

Of the eight clusters of ponds, the biggest is the Zhengyancaichi (Glamour Ponds), halfway up the valley. It

The Huanglong Hou Si was built during the Ming Dynasty.

The Gami Monastery is an influential monastery for the native Tibetan Bön religion. The mountain in the background is Xiaoxitian.

nestling harmoniously against a background of high mountains and lush forests. According to the *Annals of Songpan County*, Huanglong Rear Temple was built in the Ming Dynasty (1368–1644). First called Snow Mountain Temple, its name was changed to Huanglong Rear Temple in memory of a resident Taoist monk named Yellow Dragon who flew away after reaching immortal status. The beautiful colors of the waters in Huanglong are believed to be a gift from this monk. A unique feature of the temple is the sign over the gate, which reads differently from several angles: From the front it reads Huanglong Gu Si (Yellow Dragon Ancient Temple); from the left, it reads Fei Ge Liu Dan (Overhung Pavilion in Fluid Red); and from the right, Shan Kong Shui Bi (Clear Water in Undisturbed Mountains). An annual fair is held in front of the temple, attracting peo-

ple from hundreds of miles away to pray for good luck and successful trade.

Because the majority of the local population is Tibetan, the area around Huanglong has a number of Tibetan monasteries, including the influential Gami Si (Monastery) of the native Tibetan Bön religion. It was first built in 1355 near the source of the Minjiang (Min River) at Gonggang Ling (Ridge). Gonggang Ling is also widely known as Xiaoxitian (Lesser Eternal Paradise) Mountain, a place where souls rest after death. Because birds have been seen flying here before they die, it is also called Shadar, a Tibetan word meaning graveyard for the birds. Local Tibetans consider the mountain sacred and walk around it (a pilgrimage act called kora) every year on the fifteenth or sixteenth of the first lunar month.

Daocheng, the Last Shangri-La

In the southwestern mountains of Sichuan Province, bordering Tibet to the West and Yunnan to the South, lies a largely Tibetan county Daocheng. Its Tibetan name, Dabpa, means open land at the mouth of a valley. It is an apt description of this area of pristine natural wonders. One of its towns, Riwa, has in fact been renamed Shangri-La in an effort to compete with the better known Shangri-La County (or Zhongdian) in Yunnan. It is claimed as the authentic inspiration for the arcadia described in *Lost Horizons* by James Hilton. The argument over which location is truly Shangri-La may never be resolved. Evidently, Hilton based his Shangri-La on a story in *National Geographic* by the Austrian botanist and explorer Joseph Rock. Daocheng, however, with its stunning snowcapped peaks, hidden valleys, highland pastures, glaciers, alpine lakes, historical lamaseries and unique botany, fits the picture of the legendary paradise.

The Haizishan (Lake Mountain) Nature Reserve dominates the northern part of the county. Its 1,145 alpine

The Red Grass Marsh is the most photographed site in Daocheng.

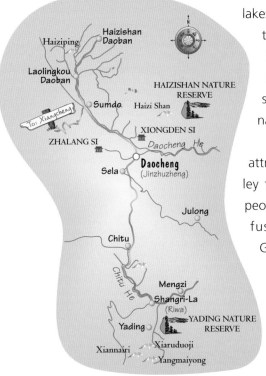

lakes are scattered over a glacier-eroded terrain. Commonly called "the old ice cap of Daocheng," the nature reserve has become an important scientific center for studying quaternary glaciers.

The small town of Sumdo is a big attraction in Daocheng. It sits in a valley full of rhododendrons, buttercups, peonies and daisies that all bloom profusely in late spring. Sumdo's Red Grass Marsh (Hongcaotan) has become the most photographed site in Daocheng.

About 17 miles (28 km) south of Sumdo is the county seat, Jinzhuzheng (Gold Pearl Town). Travelers can stop here on their way to visit Yading Nature Reserve in Riwa or, as it is called today, Shangri-La. Due to the area's sharp topographical differences, visitors can experience all four seasons in a single day. There are three snowcapped peaks in the nature reserve: Xiannairi (or Chenresig) to the north, Yangmaiyong (or Jambe-yang) to the south and Xiaruduoji (or Chanadorje) to the east. Legend says that these mountains were named by the Fifth Dalai Lama as Avalokitesvara (or Mother Buddha), Manjuist Buddha (or Wenshu Buddha) and Vajrapani (or Buddha with Warrior's Hands), respectively. Towering some 19,000 ft. (6,000 m) above sea level, they are all considered sacred by Tibetans. The best view of the three peaks is from the Luorong Yak Farm, an idyllic alpine

pastureland where the snowy peaks set off forests, grassland, mountain brooks and waterfalls.

Daocheng has thirteen Tibetan monasteries and temples. The two best known are Xiongden Si and Gonggaling Si. Situated 13,468 ft. (4,200 m) above sea level, Xiongden Monastery houses thousands of Buddhist scriptures and figures, including a sandalwood statue of Sakyamuni presented to the monastery by the Ninth Panchan Lama. Gonggaling Monastery is known for an exquisite copper statue of the bodhisattva Maitreya (the future Buddha), believed to have been presented by the Fifth Dalai Lama. Zhalang Si (Monastery) is also worth visiting for its beautiful murals and well-preserved architectural features.

Autumn foliage is set off by the snow-covered mountains in Yading (left). A skilled engraver carves out the Mani prayer stones (below).

Siguniang Shan

The pristine landscapes of western Sichuan Province have been discovered by travelers in the last dozen or so years. Danba is appreciated for its lovely valley and Tibetan watchtowers; Hailuogou, for its glaciers; Miyaluo, for its ancient Qiang villages and autumn colors; Xingduqiao, for its clear streams, undulating mountains, birch trees and grasslands dotted by Tibetan houses; and Siguniang Shan (Four Sister Mountains), for a group of four peaks that stand side by side in the middle of the Qionglai Mountain Range.

Originally called Kula Shidak, abode of the mountain god in Tibetan, Siguniang Shan marks a steep transition between the lowland Sichuan Basin and the high Tibetan plateau. Of the four peaks, Yaomei (the youngest sister) Peak is the highest, at 20,506 ft. (6,250 m) above sea level, and is widely considered the queen of Sichuan's mountains.

Although it is surrounded by towering mountains, Siguniang Shan is only 137 miles (220 km) from the

The snowcapped peaks of Siguniang Shan are visible from the Changping (left) and Haizi (opposite) valleys.

provincial capital, Chengdu. The road is in surprisingly good condition, except for a section between the city of Dujiangyan, which is known for its 2,000-year-old weir, and the small town of Yinxiu. From Yinxiu, the road winds through a lush valley along a tributary of the Minjiang (Min River), passing a few small hydroelectric plants and local villages. About halfway from Yinxiu to Siguniang Shan, there is a natural panda reserve called Wolong.

When the road starts to move away from the stream, trees are replaced by a lush carpet of grass and wildflowers that soon give way to rocky outcrops. Once across the Balang Mountain Pass, the road descends into a wide grassland area, where the snowcapped peaks of the Four Sisters are visible in the distance on a good day. Before arriving in the town of Rilong, which serves as home base for visitors to the area, look for Maobiliang or Cat's Nose Ridge, where you can get a wonderful panoramic view of of Siguniang Shan.

The sights at Siguniang Shan include glaciers, meadows, dense forests, alpine lakes and bubbling brooks, scattered in three valleys: Shuangqiao (Twin Bridge) Valley, Changping (Long Flat) Valley and Haizi (Lake) Valley. Of the three valleys, Shuangqiao provides the most views, such as Wuse Shan (Five-Color Mountain), Penjing Tan (Bonzai Bay), Renshenguoping (Ginseng Berry Meadow) and thickets of sea buckthorn, an ancient plant believed to date back hundreds of millions of years.

The peaks of Siguniang Shan are shrouded by mists and clouds in the distance (opposite). Kushutan in the Changping Valley literally means "dead tree shoal."

Wheat and barley are the major crops grown here (right).

Changping, on the other hand, must be visited on horseback or on foot. Its valley leads to the base of the Four Sisters, but very few travelers go that far because it involves camping overnight in the valley. A more popular option is to hike along a boardwalk trail that takes you through lush forests along a gushing creek, with occasional glimpses of the summit of the Four Sisters through the trees. The boardwalk ends at Kushutan, where a grove of dead pines stand in the middle of the stream. The best places in Changping to view the Four Sisters are either near the head of the trail where a wooden bridge crosses a clear brook or at Erdaoping, a small flat slope about an hour's hike.

The third valley, Haizi, is the least developed and therefore the most challenging. But it offers the closest views of the four peaks of Siguniang Shan. Haizi has a dozen or more unspoiled alpine lakes. Professional trekkers have explored the whole valley on foot and climbed its highest peaks, but most travelers are happy to visit Dahaizi (Big Lake) and Huahaizi (Colored Lake) on horseback.

Tibetan houses are usually painted every year (left). A hand-built bridge is part of a hiking trail in Changping Valley (opposite).

Famed Beauties of
Danba and the Badi Valley

Deep in the mountains of western Sichuan Province not far from the town of Danba is a valley where local Tibetans, mostly of the Jiarong group, have lived a secluded life for many centuries. Until a few years ago, there were no paved roads to this mountainous area. Remoteness allowed these Tibetans, believed to have settled here in the thirteenth century after the Xixia Kingdom along the Silk Road was destroyed, to peacefully farm this land along the Dadu He, a major tributary to the Yangtse River.

This is called the Badi Beauty Valley because the women who live here radiate such natural beauty. Their glowing good looks, despite exposure to sun and hard work, are attributed to the clean environment here as well as their royal inheritance. A local festival called Fengqing Jie (Gyarong Beauty Festival), is held in Danba every year in October, when a Khampa queen is selected from the winners of different villages.

The houses in these ancient Tibetan villages are con-structed of rock and wood and are painted black, red and white. Usually three stories high, the houses are built on sunny slopes by the river. The design of the houses is very practical: the bottom floor stables domestic animals; the middle floor is the family living area; and the top floor is used for storing grain and worshipping. There is a room on the third floor for the family to burn incense and make food sacrifices to idols for protection.

Another distinct feature of the Jiarong villages is the high watchtowers. Built of stone slabs and wood, they are scattered throughout the settlements along the Dadu River. The village of Suopo has more than eighty polygonal watchtowers, either square, pentagonal, octagonal or with as many as thirteen sides. Some of these watchtowers are one thousand years old; these fortress-like structures were first built as long ago as the Han Dynasty (206 BC–AD 220). Varying in height from 32 ft. (10 m) to 200 ft. (60 m), the watchtowers, which are sometimes attached to houses but more often stand alone, are used mainly for storing food and supplies. In peacetime, families pray for their well-being in the tow-

The watchtowers in Danba (opposite) were either attached to the Tibetan houses or stood alone.

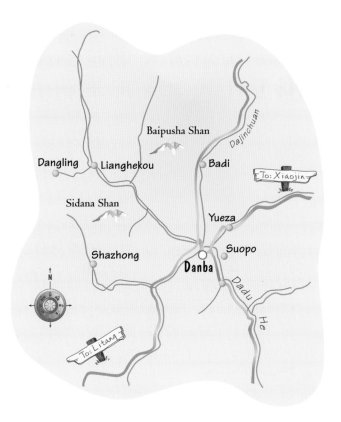

and animal species, and a natural museum of geological history. The area's thirty or more alpine lakes, yet to be explored and made accessible, rival the beauty of those in Jiuzhaigou (Nine Village Valley), which tend to be overcrowded because of their fame.

ers; in war, families used them for defense and to transmit signals to their allies from high windows.

The town of Danba is a good stopping-off point for tours of the area. Located at the point where the Bayan Har and Gonglai mountains converge, it is surrounded by snowcapped mountains, such as Murduo Mountain, the most sacred mountain for the Jiarong Tibetans, and the Dangling Range which has twenty-eight peaks with an elevation of more than 16,400 ft. (5,000 m). A sharp topographical difference in altitude—a rise of 8,825 ft. (2,690 m) within 14 miles (22 km), from the east end of the valley at Lianghekou, or Mouth of Twin River, to the summit—creates a unique environment for rare plants

The beauty of Danba women (above) is well-known, while the beauty of Clabash Lake in Dangling was only discovered recently (opposite).

Scenic and Historic
Wulingyuan

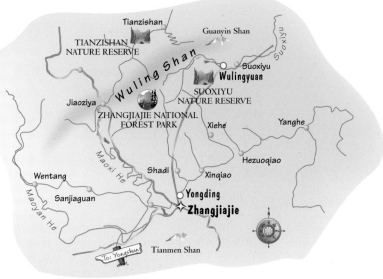

In a remote area of Hunan Province the mountain peaks and stone pinnacles of Wulingyuan (also known as Zhangjiajie National Forest Park) have remained unsung by generations of connoisseurs of the dramatic mist-draped scenes that have long been a major theme of Chinese landscape painting. While it is true that during the Qing Dynasty generals of the Yang family were sent to the region to protect China from invasion and the area is called land of the Yangs, the isolation of this part of Hunan has meant that the region was only rediscovered by the outside world in the 1970s. Interest in the region grew in the next decade when China included Wulingyuan on its list of protected national scenic areas. In the 1990s Wulingyuan gained international recognition as a World Heritage Site, and it was added to the UNESCO list of World Geological Parks.

The beautiful pinnacles are just the most visible feature of the fascinating geology here. Below ground the forces of nature have created dozens of limestone caves found in the Suoxiyu Valley and Tianzishan (Emperor

Mountain) regions. A particularly fine example is Yellow Dragon Cave, a huge limestone cavern with a natural vaulted ceiling over 150 ft. (46 m) high.

The nearly 200 sq. miles (518 sq. km.) of Wulingyuan encompasses varied terrain. Areas of dense forest shelter a number of rare and endangered species. The macaque monkey and a type of giant salamander favor the vast secluded reaches of the park. But it is the towering pinnacles, grotesque rock formations, ravines and gorges that provide endless stimulation for the imagination of the visitor. Water is ever present in countless springs, streams, waterfalls and lakes that thread the rocky complexities of the area. Abundant water is vital for the hardy pine trees that decorate many of the pin-

Water rushes through the Jinbianxi (Gold Whip Creek) at Wulingyuan (opposite).

nacles. These magnificent pines would inspire any bonsai fancier with their tenacity in this rocky environment. Pine trees occupy sites where it seems impossible for a tree to thrive. They sprout from pinnacle tops, cling gracefully to sheer sides and find footholds in the countless rock crevices. Deep in the shady ravines and gorges luxuriant moss blankets the cliffs, and ancient vines twist and cling to any available surface. The glorious blend of dramatic rock formations and tenacious vegetation seems to be nature's grandest example of the art of rock gardening.

All this rocky grandeur is rarely fully revealed because of the climatic conditions of the area. The mists that curtain the view are almost always present, thickening and obscuring everything in white fog. Suddenly winds can change the scene and tear apart the mist, shredding it to trailing ribbons that drape the landscape with torn veiling. At other times subtle air currents create rivers of mist that cascade over rocky peaks. The charm of the ever-changing atmospherics add a special enchantment to a place of great wonder.

The pinnacles range in shape from simple pillars of stone to forms suggesting the characters from China's rich storehouse of myth. Here in a grouping of stone are Piggy and his companions from the famous Journey to the West. There is a pinnacle shaped like the golden whip left carelessly behind when the first emperor of China moved mountains to fill the sea. Parted lovers, happy couples and fairy pagodas are a small sample of the shapes carved by wind, water and erosion.

Early morning mists cling and swirl around pinnacles (right).

Arcadia of the Orient—Taohuayuan

A famous Chinese bard Tao Yuanming once stumbled onto a small winding path hidden in a peach orchard. That hidden path led him to a secluded village that later became known as China's Arcadia.

The essay Tao wrote more than 1,500 years ago describes a village where time stands still, and self-reliant villagers have lost contact with the outside world. The reclusive environment preserved their traditional ways for hundreds of years after their ancestors sought refuge in this natural habitat, far away from wars and political turbulence that had engulfed the rest of China. Tao's portrait of the village, Taohuayuan, which literally means the origins of a peach orchard, establishes an enduring image of an arcadia as familiar to the Chinese as Plato's epic Atlantis.

The Chinese Arcadia is near the northeastern city of Changde in central Hunan Province. Villagers living in Taohuayuan today are surrounded by highways and resort hotels, but they have managed to convert the entire area into a gated tourist park, encompassing a peach orchard, an ancient Qin Dynasty Village and Tao-yuan Mountain.

During the last half of March when the peach trees blossom, their tender pink flowers dot the hillsides. But

Pink peach blossoms are a trademark for Taohuayuan (opposite). The 3,832-ft. (1,168-m) -long bamboo corridor (right) meanders along the foothill in what is known as the Qin Dynasty Village.

the most magnificent moment comes in the summer and fall when the evening sun displays glorious colors over the horizon of the Taoyuan Mountain and its shadows reflect upon a running creek.

The Qin Dynasty Village is accessible through a 220-ft. (67-m) long tunnel. Once inside the village, visitors will find an abundance of Qin Dynasty architecture adorned with steep curved roofs and pagodas. The most outstanding feature, however, is a 3,832-ft. (1,168-m) -long corridor held together by an extensive bamboo structure that snakes its way through the entire village.

Sanqing Shan
and Its Taoist Legacy

Sanqing Shan draws its name of Pure Trinity Mountains from the soaring peaks of Yujing, Yuxu and Yuhua which look like the three Taoist gods, Yuqing, Shangqing and Taiqing. The Taoist tradition here goes as far back as the East Jin Dynasty (AD 317–420), when the first Taoist monks came to Sanqing to build temples and practice alchemy in their search for the elixir of immortality. Among the early Taoists was a famous practitioner of Chinese medicine, Ge Hong.

For centuries, Sanqing Shan has been an important Taoist site. Its heyday was during the Ming Dynasty (1368–1644) when Emperor Zhu Yuanzhang, who had been a monk in his early years, appointed a supreme master of the Taoist religion. He also made the neighboring Taoist mountains, Longhu Shan (Dragon and Tiger Mountains), the center of Taoism in China. Taoist influence later waned after it was replaced by Buddhism as the leading religion in China during the eighteenth-century Qing Dynasty. Today, however, you can still see Sanqing's past glory in the remains of the Sanqing Palace, a Taoist temple; the five-story pentagon-shaped Fenglei Stone Pagoda; carved stone statues of Taoist gods and various cliff carvings.

Tucked into the Huaiyu Mountains of northeast

Jiangxi Province, Sanqing Shan is sometimes overshadowed by the neighboring Huang Shan (Yellow Mountain) to the north and the Wuyi Mountains to the south, both named World Heritage sites. Sanqing Shan also competes for visitors with five other national scenic areas within a radius of less than 130 miles (200 km). But its natural beauty and cultural legacy make it a worthwhile destination for travelers.

The tranquil beauty of the entire Taoist holy land was rediscovered in the early 1980s, when it was declared a national scenic area. Its mountains are surrounded with clouds and mists and covered with pine forests and intriguing rock outcroppings. The whole area can be covered on foot in two to three days. There are two loops starting from the entrance of the scenic area. The inner loop, geared to early risers, passes through exotic-shaped rocks, a sea of clouds, sunrise views and massed azaleas in the southern part of the area. The outer loop winds though Yujing Feng (Peak), Sanqing Gong (Temple) and Xihai'an (West Coast) areas for a view of mountain peaks, great sunsets, pine forests and ancient pagodas. Another wonderful hike is along the boardwalk in the West Coast. Built over a cliff, this 2-mile (3.5-km) -long trail gives you a splendid evening view of pine, birch and maple trees, azaleas, spectacular sunset viewing and ever-changing evening colors.

The port of entry for this area is Jingdezhen, capital of China's porcelain industry for the last 1,700 years. Visitors can include a stop at its ancient kilns and the porcelain museum.

Splendid views can be enjoyed from the West Coast boardwalk.

Longhu Shan,
Cradle of Taoism

Like Sanqing Shan, Longhu Shan (Dragon and Tiger Mountains) is a sacred Taoist site, 93 miles (150 km) southwest of Sanqing Shan. Its name comes from the Taoist legend of a blue dragon and white tiger suddenly appearing when the founder of Taoism, Zhang Daoling, produced the elixir of immortality. Longhu Shan is considered the cradle of Chinese Taoism. Its scenic sites cover an area of 77 sq. miles (200 sq. km) along the tranquil Luxi He (River), which meanders like a silver thread through the area's jagged red limestone rocks and sheer cliffs. Bamboo rafting down the river is a comfortable way to enjoy the amazing sights.

A raft trip starts at Shangqing Gong (Temple), whose past splendor can only be gleaned from its ruins and a Yuan Dynasty (1279–1368) bronze bell. One can get a sense of Shangqing Gong's style by visiting the intact Tianshi Fu (Heavenly Master's Mansion) about half a mile (1 km) to the west of the temple. Tianshi Fu was the residence for generations of Taoist Tianshi, or masters.

Downstream from Shangqing Gong, the river passes through a rocky section called Ten Cannots, a series of fascinating rock formations. "The Celestial Peach that You Cannot Eat," for example, is a peach-shaped rock that has a bite out of one side; "the Jade Comb that Cannot Be Used" is a midstream rock that looks like a comb with broken teeth.

Another remarkable sight is a series of coffins suspended in the caves on steep cliffs. They are believed to date from the Spring and Autumn Period (770–476 BC). These suspended burial tombs were a tradition in some parts of southern China and form one of the best outdoor archaeological museums in China.

Bamboo rafting on the Luxi River gives supreme views of dramatic rocks (opposite and above).

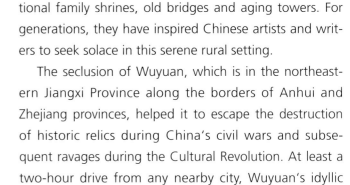

Wuyuan, Crown Jewel of the Chinese Countryside

Wuyuan, a collection of twenty small rural townships or villages in Jiangxi Province of central China, has long been known for its stunning scenery touted as the best in the Chinese countryside. These small towns or villages are nestled deep among rising mountain ridges, sloping valleys and running rivers. The villages are graced by ancient cobblestone streets, traditional family shrines, old bridges and aging towers. For generations, they have inspired Chinese artists and writers to seek solace in this serene rural setting.

The seclusion of Wuyuan, which is in the northeastern Jiangxi Province along the borders of Anhui and Zhejiang provinces, helped it to escape the destruction of historic relics during China's civil wars and subsequent ravages during the Cultural Revolution. At least a two-hour drive from any nearby city, Wuyuan's idyllic rice paddies, tea plantations and the region's signature green tea are reasons for a pause from hectic city life.

A typical Wuyuan village or town boasts a running river, flanked on both sides by graceful trees and ancient houses. Residences in Wuyuan are marked by the area's unique combination of black-tiled roofs and white walls that is commonly known as Huizhou-style architecture. A village called Xia (Lower) Xiaoqi stands out for the quiet and serenity its hills and paddies evoke in the hearts

Terraced fields are used for growing rice and tea (above and opposite).

of travelers. For a taste of historical nostalgia, Wuyuan offers an 800-year-old Rainbow Bridge and detailed carving of the Ming and Qing dynasties. This Rainbow Bridge stretches 459 ft. (140 m) and boasts of ten resting porches. A small village on the hillside by the Xinhu Lake District still maintains a matrilineal society in which the women work on the farms as the breadwinners while the men, mostly well groomed, stay at home doing household chores, taking care of the children and sipping tea in their spare time.

Beautiful and practical Rainbow Bridge (opposite) and one of the Huizhou-style villages in Wuyuan (below).

Exotic Peaks at Guifeng

Although Guifeng now means "Jade Tablet Peaks," it meant "Tortoise Peaks" in the past. This is because the characters for both names are pronounced the same way in Chinese. The older name was appropriate because the tops of these gentle mountains look like tortoises, but the new name seems more elegant.

Situated on the south bank of the Xinjiang about 6 miles (10 km) from the town of Yiyang in China's southern province of Jiangxi, Guifeng's tallest peak stands only 253 ft. (77 m) above sea level. But its strange formations, sheer cliffs and rusty red color are quite arresting to see. According to geologists, these sedimentary red sandstone peaks were formed in the Cretaceous Period (144–65 million years ago). These mountains were originally the basin of a lake and were transformed over the last eighty million years into all kinds of unusual shapes as a result of erosion and geological change.

Over the centuries, many well-known Chinese poets and scholars have paid tribute to this area, such as Wen Tingjun of the Tang Dynasty (AD 618–907) and Wang Anshi, Zhu Xi and Lu You of the Song Dynasty (AD 960–1279). The famous Ming Dynasty travel writer Xu Xiake left a detailed account of these picturesque peaks in his popular travelogue. Many of Guifeng's peaks are appropriately named for the familiar objects they resemble: Zhanqi (Unfolded Flag), Xiangya (Elephant's Tusk), Longxia (Lobster) and Matou (Horse Head). The summit of the tortoise-shaped peaks is simply called the Tortoise Peak, with a rock formation that looks like three tortoises sitting on top of each other.

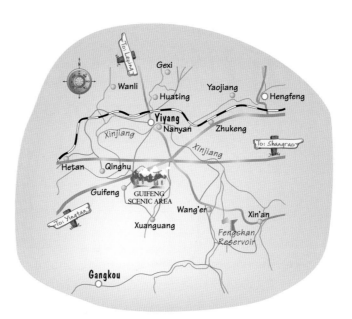

Rusty red rocks of strange formations (above and below) and their perfect reflections (opposite) in the river are a major attraction of Guifeng.

Idyllic Paradise
in a Land of Mists and Clouds

Near Huang Shan (Yellow Mountain), one of the most sacred mountains in China, lie Yixian and Shexian counties in the eastern central province of Anhui. These two counties in the traditional heartland of China boast one of the great collections of domestic architecture built in the Ming and Qing dynasties. Constructed in Huizhou style, many of these homes were built by sixteenth-century salt merchants who grew wealthy under the protection granted by the imperial government for a salt monopoly. Their wealth also permitted them to build memorial arches and ancestral halls, many of which still survive. The houses, scattered in the countryside or clustered in more than a dozen villages, typically have a courtyard surrounded on three sides by connecting buildings. The white or gray stone walls of the houses contrast strongly with beautiful sloping black-tile roofs whose practical purpose was to catch precious rainwater. Because of the rigid imperial ranking system applied to all levels of society in China during this period, even the number of courtyards a family could build was dictated by the family's rank. Some very wealthy families were allowed more than one courtyard, but most were limited to one. So it was common for ambitious families allotted only one courtyard to satisfy the desire to increase their status by applying elaborate decoration to all the structural features of the house. A walk through these Huizhou villages reveals the legacy

Huizhou villages are always situated near water.

The enduring stone and tile of Huizhou architecture.

of this restrictive imperial policy in the delightful carvings in stone, brick and wood both outside and inside the homes. Fortunately, this type of lavish decoration was not controlled by imperial edict.

In Huizhou villages houses were built close together on narrow lanes, and were further surrounded with a high crenulated wall topped with black tile. This outer wall provided security when the men of the household were away on business and also offered protection from the constant threat of fire in an era when lighting, cooking and heating were done mostly with an open flame. Usually there were two or three overhanging stories above the ground floor that were occupied by the women of the family who were often limited to observing the goings-on below in the courtyard from peepholes or small windows. Without exception, numerous streams were routed through the villages; bridges were built as part of the scheme to allow transit across the streams, ponds and canals that provided essential water to each household with such admirable ingenuity.

TAO'S DESCENDANTS

As is common in China, one or just a few family names are found in a Huizhou village; interestingly, the whole of Yixian County has a great number of families by the name of Tao. They are believed to be the descendants of Tao Yuanmin who long ago wrote a famous essay in praise of this beautiful region titled, "On Paradise," or "On the Land of the Peach Blossoms." The differences in the two titles result from the fact that literature written centuries ago is often open to interpretation. There seems to be no disagreement about the theme of a number of ancient documents that record the efforts of Tao ancestors to find a peaceful land to settle far from the chaos and violence of warfare that had driven them to this region many generations before. The centuries-old literary praises have not been forgotten, and to this day local residents often hang plaques in their villages decorated with the characters for "home in paradise."

Another tradition still found in the two counties is the growing of peach trees, which are found everywhere in household gardens and cultivated in nearby fields. A distinct feature of all Chinese villages, but highly decorated in the Huizhou style in this region, are the ancestral halls that served families with the same last name as a ceremonial meeting place to honor ancestors,

as a place to conduct family business and, in some cases, as a place of study for the annual imperial exams, the results of which play an important role in determining one's career.

MEMORIAL ARCHES

At the entrance of and sometimes even inside a Chinese village, memorial arches were often erected to honor a special event, the emperor or a famous person. Happily, many of these arches have survived in the Huizhou villages. Some of the most interesting series of arches were the product of successive generations of one family. For example, in nearby Shexian County, although there are a total of ninety-four arches, seven of them were built over a period of four hundred years by the Bao family of salt merchants. Another striking example is the 33-ft. (10-m) -high arch built in the late sixteenth century with local dark gray stone. The archway commemorates the then governor of the Jiao Prefecture. It is guarded by magnificent carved lions and embellished with eagles, pheasant tails and more lions frolicking with embroidered balls.

In addition to carving in a variety of materials, Huizhou-style buildings often have wooden architectural details painted in what were once bright colors. Between carving and painting, a complete catalogue of favorite Chinese pictorial symbols cover the many surfaces that the Huizhou salt merchants gloried in deco-

Carved screens and lintels in the main hall of a Yixian dwelling (opposite). One of the memorial arches in Xidi Village (right).

rating. Everywhere there are real and imagined animals such as phoenixes, lions and the Chinese unicorn called a qilin. Other motifs include flowers and birds, scenes of farming, processions of all types and even the famous Confucian twenty-four examples of filial piety.

The three-sided courtyard houses, walled all around, and all with extravagant surface decoration are just the most evident aspects of the Huizhou villages, but there is more to see in these precious survivors of China's history. The terrain of the region is quite hilly, and amazingly it is only by viewing the villages from above that one can truly appreciate the way houses were carefully situated in the available space near rivers and ponds. In Hongchun (Hong Village), the outline of the village resembles a water buffalo resting on its side, and the lanes, streams and ponds correspond to parts of the dozing animal. Much has been made of the characteristics of water buffaloes influencing the character and strength of Hongchun and its inhabitants, and tradition holds that the planned layout was the result of consultations with feng shui masters long ago. The spectacular ponds, one a lily pond with a lovely arched bridge, and the other a crescent-shaped pond famed for its beautiful reflections, have made Hongchun (see photo, pages 174–175) a World Heritage site.

To the southwest lies Nanping Village, which has the unusual architectural feature of house corners bowed in so as to avoid the shape of a sharp point. The standard type of corners seemed to symbolize potential discord among villagers. The idea was to remove even the archi-

Residential houses in Nanping Village (opposite).

tectural suggestion of neighbors quarreling. Even though the village is well laid out, the thirty-six wells and seventy-two interlocking lanes make for a fascinating maze to wander about.

It may take more time to tour each of the Huizhou villages than most visitors can spare. Certainly their fame is justified, and several Huizhou villages were used in the movie "Crouching Tiger, Hidden Dragon", and by the Chinese movie director, Zhang Yimou. But there is a way to appreciate and absorb the impact of Yixian's or Shexian's fabulous treasure houses in just one place: Qiankou Village with its wonderful collection of Huizhou-style buildings that represent the rich variety of the region. It is a day trip that will reward, educate and delight any visitor to China.

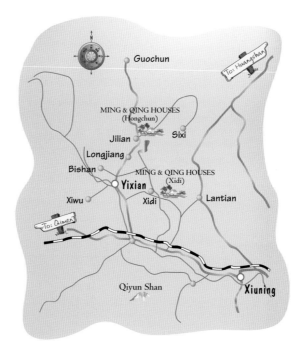

Huizhou-Style
Houses in Shexian County

Houses in southern Anhui Province have a distinct architecture known as Huizhou style. The homes were mostly built in the Ming and Qing dynasties, featuring dark gray tiles, white walls, elaborately shaped eaves, exquisite engravings of flowers, geometric patterns on blue stone parapets and colored paintings on the beams, lintels and door frames, typical of the area that was once called Huizhou or Hui Prefecture. Shexian County was once the government seat for Huizhou, and it is still referred to as the Old Huizhou Seat by the local population.

Surrounded by mountains and yet not too far from the political and cultural centers of China, this little county of 1,042 sq. miles (2,700 sq. km) has always been considered a peaceful paradise in periods of upheaval and war. Though 95 percent of the region is mountainous and not the best agricultural land, Shexian County is historically home to a great number of successful scholars and merchants. For more than 500 years

in the Ming and Qing dynasties, the Hui merchants were one of the influential merchant groups in China. Salt was an important commodity for trade. Mild climate and abundant rain has created excellent conditions for tea and fruit trees. Rare species of flowers have thrived in Huizhou as well. Its idyllic natural beauty inspired the well-known Ming Dynasty playwright Tang Xianzhu to write of his "infatuation" with Huizhou.

The great number of Huizhou families successful in government careers and trade is reflected in the well-preserved Ming and Qing style buildings that had rich detail lavished on them by their prosperous owners. The buildings include residences and family ancestral halls. There are also stone bridges, memorial arches (erected with the approval of the emperor) and chastity arches for women who were considered models of traditional virtues. The area is an outdoor museum of domestic architecture and civic art.

Of these structures, the stone pagodas of Xingzhou and Changqing Temple are from the Song Dynasty (AD

Zhushan Academy (opposite) in Shexian County, home of many scholars.

Courtyard of a residence in Tangyue Village (left) and a set of memorial arches outside the village (above).

960–1279), while the Xuguo Stone Archway was erected in 1584 under the reign of Wanli of the Ming Dynasty. The three stone bridges, Taiping, Shoumin and Wannian, were also built in the same era. But the most impressive is the group of seven memorial arches outside the village of Tangyue. These arches (there were once 250 of them all over the county) are three-dimensional history books that guide visitors to an appreciation of the culture and history of this quiet little town in central China.

The Water Town of
Tongli

Near the famous water town of Suzhou in Jiangsu Province, Tongli is one of a number of small towns built around canals fed by the system of lakes and rivers in the rich Yangtze River Delta. The long settled area is crisscrossed with waterways including the ancient Grand Canal, now no longer navigable in many parts, but built long ago to connect the center of power in the north of China with the riches of the south.

For convenience Tongli households are built next to waterways rather than streets. There are fifteen rivers that meander through Tongli and forty-nine bridges cross them. The riverbeds have been carefully re-arranged as they pass through Tongli, and this divides the town into seven xu (section). Built over an extended period beginning in the Song Dynasty, the bridges joining each section of Tongli are either flat or arched, but all the bridges lead onto the town's narrow paved streets. Careful inspection of the bridges often reveals the date of construction carved into the stones.

Houses were built next to waterways in the water town of Tongli (opposite). The interior of Tuisi Garden of the Qing Dynasty (right).

Most houses in Tongli have a stairway or dock to reach the water used for household tasks or for boarding boats. Although there are wells and running water to homes in Tongli, most households continue to enjoy the sociability provided by performing the domestic tasks of food preparation and washing on the stairways and docks of their waterways.

The long history of Tongli is evident from the many Ming and Qing dynasty buildings in the town. Tongli also boasts numerous writers, artists and scholars who have placed well in the grueling imperial exams. Scattered throughout the town are a number of classic book salons where in the past people devoted to literature and the arts would gather for appreciation and discussion. It's possible that the plans for the Tuisi Garden built by Ren Nansheng in the Qing Dynasty may have been a topic of discussion at such a gathering. The garden was built after Ren's retirement from government office, a typical activity for the successful bureaucrat of the era. Within a third of an acre there was room for living quarters, pavilions, gazebos, ponds, artificial hills and archways created with charm and elegance. Today Tongli remains a place of peace and beauty.

Houses in Tongli are built along the waterways (left). The beautiful Tuisi Garden (opposite) used to be the residence of a retired bureaucrat of the Qing Dynasty.

The Rainbow Bridge in Jinze

An intriguing experiment involving a joint effort between Chinese and American experts in building a wooden bridge in use over nine hundred years ago was completed in the small town of Jinze near Shanghai several years ago. The inspiration for the project was a bridge pictured in a famous twelfth-century scroll of the ancient city of Kaifeng. Easy to identify from the scroll was the camelback configuration of the bridge typical of the time period; more difficult to grasp were the bridge's structural details.

Working with American television producers of a PBS series titled "Secrets of the Lost Empires," Professor Tang Huancheng, an engineer and writer on historical Chinese bridges, and engineering professor Yang Shijin of Tonji University of Shanghai, designed a replica of a twelfth-century bridge called a flying or rainbow bridge. A great deal of brainstorming, analysis and model building went on both in China and at the Massachusetts Institute of Technology before construction began. Working with a local contractor, Chen Fuxiang, who supplied all the materials and the team of builders, the Chinese and U.S. teams began in 1999 to construct the bridge with the understanding that only materials available in the twelfth century would be used.

The plans followed the parameters of a local legend of a bridge built by a clever prison guard famous for his woven baskets. Ordered by the provincial governor to build a bridge, his task, much like a good puzzle, was to make a bridge using only 20-ft. (6-m) -long timbers. There were no piers since piers added great difficulty, interfered with river traffic and could be swept away by seasonal floods. It may have been that the limit of 20-ft. (6-m) -lengths for the timbers was due to the scarcity of longer timber due to deforestation.

The Rainbow Bridge in Jinze County was designed to be 50-ft. (15-m) long and 12-ft. (3.6-m) wide, with timbers forming two parallel interlocking arches, one arch with three sides, and the other with four. All joints were bound with specially braided bamboo rope. Glue would not be used to avoid retaining moisture around the timbers. Rot-resistant larch timbers were chosen for the job. Only tung oil, a natural preservative available in the twelfth century, was used to treat the timbers after construction.

It was finally agreed that the bridge would be assembled elsewhere in two halves and be brought to the site, then carefully lowered in place with the help of a scaffolding erected on two boats stationed in the canal. The bridge's granite abutments were put in place with the aid of a twelfth-century-style cofferdam built of a clay wall between two bamboo forms. All the water was removed by hand before building the stone abutments. Although the original rainbow bridge used only bamboo lashing, the local contractor insisted on galvanized steel bolts. This would not meet the project's requirement of twelfth-century materials and methods, but wrought iron had been used by the Chinese in bridge building

The reconstruction of a twelfth-century wooden bridge was a joint effort by a Chinese-US team.

since the sixth century, and so finally split iron nails were used.

Load testing included the use of two large water buffaloes driven over the bridge. Once open for foot traffic, the townspeople of Jinze welcomed the beauty and convenience of their new bridge with a great celebration complete with fireworks.

Xiandu,
a Fairy Land

The scenic area of Xiandu in the eastern central province of Zhejiang has attracted visitors since well before the Tang Dynasty over a thousand years ago. Long ago Chinese writers visiting the area praised in verse the unusual rock formations, cliffs and deep gorges. In several locations ancient calligraphy, a high art in China, is carved in huge characters on rock walls in honor of the dramatic scenery. The name of the area comes from a report long ago to the Tang emperor Xuanzhong of colorful, holy clouds complete with heavenly music gracing the mountaintops. The emperor, amazed at the report, personally wrote the two characters Xian Du, meaning "Fairy Town," and dedicated this title to a place with the landscape that seems to have its own celestial musical accompaniment.

The Chinese penchant for inventing poetic titles is evident in Xiandu. One peak alone, Dinghu Peak, has four competing names, all delightfully picturesque. How could anyone choose just one name when Jade Bamboo Shoot Peak, Red Mineral Peak, Stone Bamboo Peak and

Dinghu Peak towers above a small lake in Xiandu.

Solitary Peak have all been used to describe this 500-ft. (152-m) -tall rock formation that seems to sprout in complete isolation from the bank of a river. In an old legend explaining the name of the peak, the Emperor Huang was said to have built, on the flat top of Dinghu Peak, a bronze ding, a three-legged cauldron used in early Chinese civilization for ceremonial purposes. Using the ding he refined the red mineral of the area until he could consume the mineral's essence. The emperor then flew to heaven on a dragon's back. The story continues that the ding, left behind by the emperor, was used to pound the top of the rock formation until a tiny lake was created, and so the name Dinghu means Ding Lake. Much later, Yuan Meisheng, a writer of the Qing Dynasty exclaimed about the famous peak, "nothing around as beautiful; lofty, high, and worshiped." In tribute to the sublime beauty of Xiandu, three of the most famous sites have huge works of calligraphy carved into the rock proclaiming their magnificence. Xiandu deserves the title of "the number one stone under heaven."

There are a number of other sites that draw visitors, such as Dongzi Peak, Xianshui Cave and Mount Buxu where the Guanhu (Lake View) Pavilion affords a splendid view of Dinghu Peak. Yet another location memorialized by a giant rock calligraphy is Tiemen (or Iron Gate) Gorge. The steep reddish cliffs on either side come to such a narrow divide that only one horse can pass at a time. "Old Man Ni's Ravine" is inscribed into the rock in honor of the hermit Ni that legend says once inhabited in the caves. Surely the old hermit must have watched from one of his caves, as a visitor can to this day, to see the sun rising above the opposite hill called

Poxi Crag with the daughter-in-law kneeling before her mother-in-law.

Mount Horse Saddle. This dawn view from the cave also has the descriptive and fanciful title of "unbridled horse carrying the sun."

Another delightfully named scenic site in Xiandu is Lone Peak School, the place where the famed scholar Zhu Xi taught, and which is still the location for a school built in the Qing Dynasty. The mountain behind the school has a gigantic hole near the peak that has been compared both to a bright moon on a dark night and a mirror. Moon and Mirror is the name of this unusual peak. Near Old Man Ni's Ravine above Haoxi (Hao Creek) is a cliff called Lesser Chibi that is dotted with crevices and hollows that water pours from in a silvery screen. In the creek are several tiny islands from where one can see the Poxi Crag in the distance, resembling a very old mother-in-law standing across from her kneeling daughter-in-law.

The Southern Region

The Ancient Town of Shigu at the First Bend in the Yangtze

Shigu is a historic small town 31 miles (50 km) from the well-known city of Lijiang. It sits near a shallow section of the Yangtze River where it flows north after its great bend. This part of the Yangtze River is called Jinshajiang or Gold Sand River, because gold was once found there. It is one of the three parallel rivers that gush along the deep gorges of the Hengduan Shan Range, a north-south chain that borders three southwestern Chinese provinces: Yunnan, Sichuan and Tibet.

Shigu means stone drum and the town is named after a stone tablet shaped like a drum that records the heroism of a local leader who fended off Tufan (or Tubo) invasions twice between 1515 and 1568. Shigu has been a strategically important town throughout its history. The famous Chinese strategist of the Three Kingdoms period (AD 220–280), Zhuge Liang, chose to cross the Yangtze here. So did Kublai Khan during his southern expedition in the thirteenth century and the Chinese Communist Army on its long march to the North in 1936. Shigu was also once an important trading post for the Tibetans and Han Chinese, and a stop on the tea and horse trade route.

History is reflected in Shigu's cobblestone streets and well-preserved buildings, as well as a chain-link bridge called Tiehong (Iron Rainbow) that was originally built in 1885 over a tributary of the Jinshajiang.

The Yangtze makes a U-turn near the town of Shigu (opposite), where a stone tablet was built in honor of a heroic village leader (below).

*L*ugu Lake,
Home to a Matriarchal
Society

According to the Old Tang Book, there was a matriarchal tribe of Dongnu (eastern women) who resided 1,000 years ago in the area of present-day Chamdo, in the eastern highlands of Tibet. Some of them moved eastward after their tribe was destroyed by the Tufan. The ancestors of the Mosuo people who live around the beautiful Lugu Hu (Lake) on the border of Yunnan and Sichuan provinces are believed to have been part of this large-scale migration.

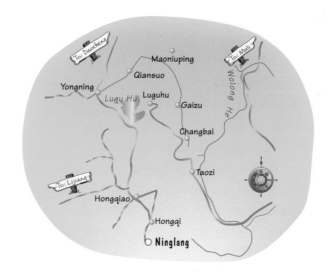

The Mosuo still live in a matriarchal society. Rather than conventional marriages, Mosuo men and women have a relationship called "axia." An adult can have more than one axia, or dear companion, in his or her life, but not at the same time. Mosuo men work at home during the day but spend the night with their axias, if the women agree. Children are looked after by their maternal families. When an adult relationship is terminated, the children usually continue to live with their mother. When a new axia relationship becomes serious, the couple can live together either with the woman's or man's family. This is called "azhu." A girl becomes adult when she is thirteen years old. After an initiation ceremony, she can wear skirts instead of long gowns and is free to choose her axia.

Mosuo women are historically among the most liberated females that ever lived. They ruled their tribe for centuries. Although life is changing in this isolated area, its rich feminist heritage is still evident.

Lugu Lake offers lovely beaches and bays. The best way to explore the lake and its five islands is by rowing

A young Mosuo woman in her finery (right).

around it in a local "pig-trough" boat. Three of the islands are compared to the legendary Three Islands of Penglai (the Land of the Immortals).

The Mosuo religion is called Daba, a combination of ancient nature worship and Tibetan Buddhism. Every year the Mosuo make a religious circuit around their sacred mountain, the Gemu, on the twenty-fifth day of the seventh lunar month. On that day they dress in their finest clothes for the sacrificial rites of worshipping their goddess. It is also an occasion for dancing, archery contests and for young people, looking for their axias.

A sturdy pig-trough boat (above) is a convenient transportation vehicle for getting around Lugu Lake (right).

Shangri-La in Yunnan Province

The northwestern corner of Yunnan Province is a landscape reminiscent of James Hilton's idyllic community, Shangri-La, described in his classic book *Lost Horizons*. Deep gorges with rushing rivers cut through the towering mountains and the high grasslands are dotted with mirrorlike alpine lakes.

Inhabited by a dozen ethnic groups, this peaceful region has a rich cultural history. At different times of the year, each population celebrates its own festivals, such as the Riba (drum and performance), Xunzi (a group dance accompanied by a Tibetan string instrument) and Guozhuang (campfire) dances for the Tibetans, and the Foot Tapping dances for the Lisu people (another ethnic group in the region). The area also has varied religious traditions: Tibetan Buddhism, Christianity, Dongba, Bön and Islam.

Bathing Buddha Festival takes place at Songzhanlin (above), which houses the statue of the founder of the Yellow Hat Sect (opposite, bottom).

What is referred to today as Shangri-La covers an area of over 9,000 sq. miles (23,000 sq. km) in Diqing, a Tibetan autonomous region. The government seat of this area changed its name from Zhongdian County to Shangri-La in 2001. Much of Shangri-La's landscape remains in a pristine state. Particularly beautiful are Bita and Napa lakes (see photo of Napa Lake, pages 196-197); Baishui Tai, a limestone formation; and snow-capped mountains Haba, Meimang and, especially, Meili, a mountain sacred to the Tibetans. Tibetan pilgrims have been circumambulating Meili (a pilgrimage called kora in Tibetan) for seven hundred years. The summit of Meili Mountains, Kagbo Peak, is the highest in Yunnan, soaring 22,114 ft. (6,740 m) into the sky.

Tibetans are the largest ethnic group in Shangri-La, but the populace also includes other groups such as the Naxi, Lisu and Yi. At a crossroad for the ancient tea and horse trade between Tibet, Sichuan and Yunnan, Shangri-La has an interesting cultural history. Two monasteries stand out: Dongzhulin and Songzhanlin. First built in 1679 like the Potala Palace in Lhasa, the Songzhanlin Monastery (also called Guihua Monastery)

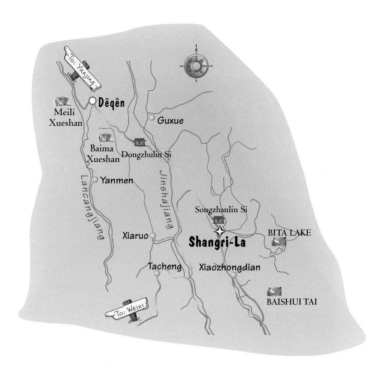

Calciferous terraces of Baishui Tai are referred to as growing flowers in the local Naxi language.

is the largest and most famous Tibetan lamasery in Yunnan. The design of the monastery incorporates both Tibetan and Han architectural features. It was named by the Fifth Dalai Lama and currently houses about seven hundred Tibetan monks.

Baishui Tai, or White Water Terrace, lies in the Zhong-jian County to the southeast of the Shangri-La County. A holy place for Naxi ceremonies, it was formed from water erosion on limestone terrain, similar to the topog-raphy in the Huanglong Scenic Area. Viewed from a dis-tance, the white limestone terraces look like solid water-falls. At closer range, they appear more like milky-white jade bathed by crystal clear water.

Life along the Three Parallel Rivers

The famous Sanjiang (Three Rivers) Gorges are dramatically deep river channels in the Hengduan Shan Range of western China. The farthest west is the Nujiang (Nu River), which later becomes the Salween in Myanmar. The middle river is the Lancangjiang. When it enters Laos, it is called the Mekong. The third river is the Jinshajiang, meaning Gold Sand River, which is the name for the upper reaches of the Yangtze River. The three rivers run parallel through the mountains, their waters rushing down narrow boulder-strewn chasms in a spectacular landscape. Each of the river valleys has a depth of more than 3,000 ft. (1,000 m).

The three river gorges follow their individual courses through fifteen counties of the Yunnan, Sichuan and Tibetan provinces. More than sixty percent of the local inhabitants are Tibetan; the rest are other ethnic groups. The Dulong, Lisu and Nu live along the Nujiang; the Naxi, Bai and Pumi live in the Lancangjiang Gorge; and the Yi people live in the Jinshajiang Gorge.

These minority groups still maintain their own customs, habits and religious beliefs. The Naxi of the Lijiang area are known for their ancient Dongba culture, passed from generation to generation by "dongbas," the wise men of this ethnic group. Their culture is rooted in the worship of supernatural gods. Additional influences have been Buddhism and Taoism. Dongba script, with more than 1,400 characters, is believed to be the world's only well-preserved living pictographic language.

The rock paintings in a village called Lasidi along the Nujiang shed light on the history of the Nu people. The Dulong people are now confined to the Dulong River Valley parallel to the Nujiang Gorge on the other side of the Gaoligong Mountains. Dulong women have a tradition of tattooing their faces.

Climate along the gorges can vary from sub-tropical in the valley bottom to arctic cold on the mountaintops that are covered by ice or snow year round. The terrain is just as varied, from warm and moist river valleys in the upper Lancangjiang to rugged mountain slopes along the Nujiang. Tibetans on the mountain slope of Meili

The highways snake along the Lancangjiang (opposite) and Jinshajiang (below) valleys.

A cane-woven net bridge (above) and steel cable bridge (far opposite) over the Nujiang (right).

grow fruits and pick medicinal herbs and mushrooms, especially a wild edible fungus similar to the French truffle. Meili in Tibetan means "medicinal herbs mountain." The Lisu people who live in the deep gorges of the Nujiang cope with a severe environment. A limited supply of flat land has conditioned them into building elevated houses with multiple supports, called "thousand legs." The elevated rooms are for human habitation; animals live down below.

High mountains and deep gorges make bridges a necessity in this area. A 186-mile (300-km) -long section of the Nujiang Gorge is appropriately called "a museum of bridges." Alongside conventional wood, chain and cement bridges, the local inhabitants have created two unique ways to cross a river: sliding across along a steel cable (like Tyrolean traverse) or walking over a cane-woven net bridge. Both require courage as well as skill.

Rape Flowers and Waterfalls in *Luoping*

People visit Luoping County in east Yunnan Province to see two things: vast fields of rape flowers in bloom and the many spectacular waterfalls. Rape flowers, which are grown for their oil-bearing seeds, are not so beautiful in small amounts. But when more than 49,000 acres (20,000 hectares) of golden rape flowers are all growing in one place, the sight is truly remarkable. With a mild climate and plenty of rain, the farmers of Luoping County have made their living for years by growing rape flowers. The annual output of rapeseed in Luoping is 66 million lb. (30 million kg), a quarter of Yunnan's total output.

It wasn't until the late 1990s that the flowers started to draw hundreds of thousands of visitors, not to mention bees and bee farmers, to Luoping every year. The sight of an endless expanse of rape flowers, dotted with interesting cone-shaped limestone outcroppings that look like islands in a yellow sea, is breathtaking. The rape flowers are at their best from late February to late March. The eastward journey from the provincial capital, Kunming, to Luoping doesn't prepare one for the full impact of miles of golden rape flowers in full bloom

until the traveler goes beyond Mount Baila. The golden fields extend for almost 20 miles (30 km) to the far horizon. Luoxiong, the county town, sits right in the middle of these endless fields, looking like a big island. Another place with a good view of the golden landscape is Jinji (Golden Rooster) Village on top of Jinji Ling (Ridge). From there you can see an amazing sight on a foggy day as the dark shapes of numerous cone-shaped limestone or karst outcroppings gradually emerge from the mist.

Calcified waterfalls are the other major attraction in Luoping. A group of ten waterfalls on Jiulong He (Nine Dragons River) is a magnificent sight. The largest is Shenlong (Holy Dragon) Waterfall with a width of more than 360 ft. (110 m). The calcified shoals, waterfalls and bamboo bridges on the Duoyi River are also quite beautiful. The Buyi, who are known for their love of water, are one of the biggest ethnic groups in the region.

The Buyi, Shui, Yi, Miao and Hui live side by side with the Han Chinese in Luoping, giving the area a rich cultural history. The Buyi are the native residents of

Cones of limestone punctuate the golden rape fields (opposite).

Luoping and have the greatest number of festivals. The most popular brings the Buyi, Shui, Yi and Zhuang from the neighboring three provinces to Jiulong He to celebrate their Singing Contest Festival on the second day of the second lunar month. Their Water Festival is celebrated on the third day of the third lunar month. Activities include bamboo-raft racing, singing contests, dancing and, most exciting of all, splashing guests with water. Colored rice and dyed eggs are served along with other local delicacies.

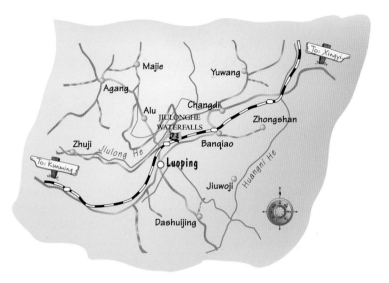

Terraced waterfalls on Jiulong He look like giant stair steps (opposite). Entertaining guests with wine is a tradition at festivals (below).

Huangguoshu
and Its Neighboring Scenic Sites

Not many people in China know where the city of Anshun is, but they know where Huangguoshu Waterfalls are. This group of eighteen falls, the largest in China with a maximum span of over 260 ft. (80 m) and a drop of around 220 ft. (67 m), lies some 28 miles (45 km) from Anshun. Although these nine-step waterfalls are actually in the county of Zhenning, Anshun has always been the favorite starting point for visiting Huangguoshu, Longgong Dong (Dragon Palace Caves) and the recently discovered Tunbao communities (garrison fortress villages).

Huangguoshu derives its name from the citrus fruit tree (below), while Tianxing Qiao is named after the natural stone bridges (right).

Huangguoshu Waterfalls derives its name from a tangerine fruit tree, common upstream along the Baishui He (White Water River), a tributary of the Beipanjiang (Beipan River). During the rainy season from May to October, water from the Baishui He thunders into the Rhinoceros Pool at the foot of the fall, creating two ponds, each more than 50 ft. (15 m) deep.

TIANXING QIAO

About 4 miles (7 km) downstream from Huangguoshu, the Baishui River runs through the recently developed Tianxing Qiao (Star Bridge) scenic area, which consists of all kinds of stone bridges, forests and caves. The area begins where the river zigzags through a valley over shallow shoals 1,148 ft. (350 m) wide before disappearing under a stone forest. The subterranean river emerges less than a mile away from the other end of the scenic area. A walk through the stone forests and caves or over the bridges is like a trip into a fairy land.

The Baishui He (River) roars at top speed before it disappears under a stone forest in the Tianxing Qiao area.

Tunbao Communities

Also found in the area are some three hundred Tunbao communities, literally the garrison fortress villages, with a population of approximately 300,000. The Tunbao inhabitants live in fortlike stone-and-wood houses on hilltops, dress like the southern Chinese of the Ming Dynasty, still perform dixi—a form of traditional drama mainly depicting war stories in ancient times—and make lanterns as offerings to their ancestors. Their way of life is different from other migrant Hans or local ethnic groups, and their dialect is that of one spoken in southern China more than six hundred years ago. They are actually the descendants of the 300,000 Han (the

Terraced fields of the Tunbao area turn golden in the fall (below). Tunbao residences are built on some of the hilltops.

For the Tunbao inhabitants, dixi is a popular drama put on by the villagers themselves.

largest ethnic group) troops, sent by the first Ming emperor, Zhu Yuanzhang, to suppress ethnic rebellions. When the battles were over, they settled down with their families, relocated here to farm the land and guard the frontier. These fortress villages are scattered over an area of 500 sq. miles (1,300 sq. km) around Anshun. The most representative are Yunshantun and Benzhai, where the inhabitants, especially the old generation, still observe some of the traditions of the Ming Dynasty and dress in Ming-style long loose gowns in sapphire blue.

The *Miao* Customs in the Miaoling Mountain Range

Southwest Guizhou Province is home to the Miaoling Mountain Range, an area favored with a mild climate and fertile soil. Pines, firs and fragrant camphor trees thrive and numerous rare plant and animal species make the mountains their home. The Miaoling Range is an area where precious medicinal herbs have long been harvested. The highest peak, Leigong Mountain in the eastern part of the range, forms part of the watershed for two of the area's most important rivers, the Yangtze and the Zhujiang. The name of the mountain range itself is said to come from the many Miao and Dong villages scattered throughout the area. Both the Miao and the Dong practice a type of terraced farming in this mountainous region.

Using knowledge gained from generations as hill farmers, the Miao villagers specialize in certain crops

Wooden frames and black-tiled roofs are typical of the Miao villages.

Festival costumes and silver headwear help to identify the villages where these women come from.

depending on location. Villages near the hilltops grow mostly corn, potatoes, buckwheat and millet. Farther down, in steep terrain or in the small valleys at the base of the hills, rice and other grains are cultivated.

In addition to perfecting farming in this mountainous region, the Miao have attracted a great deal of attention because of the women's beautiful costumes and unusual hairstyles. All girls begin learning early a number of demanding textile arts that include weaving, dyeing, batik, cross-stitch and embroidery. Visitors come to observe the production of textiles and to enjoy the festival days when all the Miao wear their distinctive dress. Preparations for the most important day in the Miao calendar, the Miao New Year, celebrated in the tenth month of the lunar calendar, go on for much of the year. This is because most of the costume, which varies

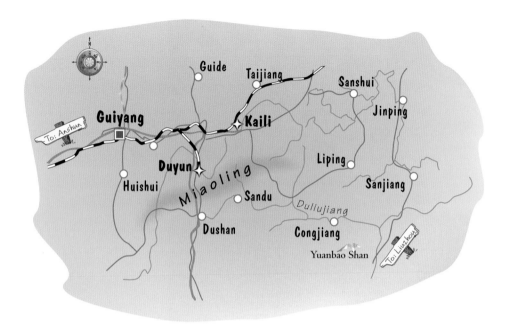

from village to village and is worn at all festivals, is made by hand. The New Year holiday combines ancestor worship with visiting family and friends. Some villages sponsor bull fights; others hold a dance accompanied by the lusheng, a musical instrument made of a large piece of bamboo. For the young people this holiday is the long-awaited chance to show off. Love and courtship are on everyone's mind. In their finest clothes, with elaborate hairdos for the young girls, the dancing and singing go on late into the evening. This chance for young people to meet, celebrate and socialize free from

This hairstyle is worn only by one group of the Miao (above). The lusheng is a popular musical instrument for the Miao and Dong (left).

the usual cares of daily existence is called Youfang, which means full of festivity, and is an opportunity for the young Miao to begin the process of finding a mate.

The fascinating variety in the decoration of costume and hairstyle of the Miao depends entirely on the village. One hairstyle involves the use of a huge buffalo comb on which is piled a large figure-eight of hair, often several pounds of treasured hair from mothers and grandmothers. Another village decorates the hairdo with pieces of candy, embroidery thread and small decorative objects. The use of coiled braids on top of the head with the rest of the hair worn loose is another Miao village variation. In yet a different village the hair is wrapped in a black scarf as a support for large wooden horns that give the appearance of a buffalo head. Wool or hemp is added when necessary to help in shaping these towering creations.

The type of skirt worn by the Miao women is also identified according to the village. Often dyed with indigo to a deep blue-black, the handwoven material is then very finely pleated and embroidered with brilliant colors, often in bands near the hem. These basic design elements are the general framework for each village to create its own recognizable variation. Some Miao skirts are just long enough to cover the knee, while others are worn ankle length. Some skirts are worn at the waist, and others are fastened at hip level. In some villages the women pile on as many as ten skirts at a time.

Villagers hang ears of corn on racks for drying.

Dong Villages
in Southern China

D escendants of one of the Baiyue tribes in southern China, the Dong people have inhabited the borders of Guangxi, Hunan and Guizhou provinces as long as anyone can remember. A typical village is made up of families all with the same family name, though larger villages may have several last names. This is important because for each family name, a drum tower must be built, usually in the center of the village. This typical Dong structure plays a pivotal role in the life of the village. Whenever there is an important issue to be discussed, the tower guard will strike a drum hanging on the second floor to call the villagers together. On cold days, village elders sit and warm themselves in front of a heating tank in the center of the first floor.

While Dong drum towers are all built of wood and dark gray tiles, each has its own architectural style; there are hall-style, pagoda-style, palace-style and pavilion-style drum towers. Some towers have five roofs, others seven, and some have as many as eleven. The Ma'an Drum Tower (right) in Sanjiang County, Guangxi, is a modest example with seven gable roofs compared to the drum tower with many more peaked roofs (see photo, page 220).

Most Dong villages sit by a river nestled against nearby hills, making bridges a necessity. Dong bridges are unique. They are covered and combine the features of bridge, corridor and pavilion. Some of them are called Fengyu Qiao (Wind and Rain Bridge); others are called Hua Qiao (Flower Bridge). No matter the style, the bridges provide more than a passage across the river;

The Dong villages in Sanjiang County, Guangxi (opposite).

Each drum tower is different in the Dong villages (left).
The interior (above) and exterior (opposite) of Huilong Bridge in
Tongdao County, Hunan Province, is typical of Dong architecture.

they also offer a comfortable resting place and shelter against the wind and rain, common during the planting and harvesting seasons.

Huilong (Dragon Turning Its Head) Bridge is typical of the Dong bridge architecture. Originally built in 1761, it spans a small stream in Tongdao County, southwestern Hunan. (The current structure dates back to 1931.) The bridge, 262 ft. (80 m) long, 13 ft. (4 m) wide, is constructed entirely of pine. All the joints are dovetailed, so there is not one nail in the whole structure. The bridge

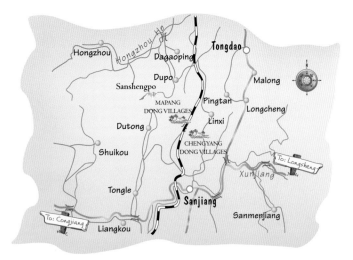

consists of two sections. The western section rests on several layers of beams, which are placed one above the other and cantilevered out on both ends to distribute the weight of the bridge on the pier below. The eastern section rests on beams, which in turn are supported by wooden blocks that sit on the brick pier. The covering is a double-eaved, wood-tiled roof.

The Dong have a population of 1.5 million and are mostly farmers and foresters. They also have a reputation for great artistry. The Dong women are skilled

Dong women sing during a festival in their finest dress and silver jewelry.

weavers who make intricately patterned brocades that are both beautiful and durable. The Dong are also noted for their folk theater and music played on wind instruments of their own design, the liukong and shuchui.

Of the many festivities in Sanjiang County, the Dong marriage procession is of particular interest, especially the one called Song Xinniang (Escort the Bride Home). Dong marriages are usually held on the second day of the first lunar month. The next day the bridegroom's family escorts the bride back to her parents with gifts, such as pigs, rice and wine. This procession is accompanied by firecrackers and, more often than not, it takes the longest possible route to show off the wealth of the bridegroom and his family.

Singing also plays a great part in Dong life, from simple occasions such as choosing a young village girl or urging a guest to extend his stay by singing what is called a blocking the road song, to the serious business of courtship and marriage. For example, a Dong bridegroom will usually lead his male attendants in singing to the girls attending the bride on his wedding day as they walk together to the bride's family home. Only after this singing dialogue is performed satisfactorily can the groom bring his new bride home.

Since the Dong grow both rice and corn, they have combined the two grains in a delicious and fragrant concoction called butter rice porridge. Made with a mixture of glutinous rice, corn, popcorn and a local butter substitute, it is a famous dish in the region.

Simple wooden bridges (right) are used inside the village, in addition to the elaborate "wind and rain" bridges.

The Magnificent
Terraced Fields of
Longsheng

In Longsheng County near the famous city of Guilin, a gigantic mosaic of endless terraces seems to lead straight up to the sky on Yuecheng Mountain. Built over many generations, these terraced fields are used for growing rice. The astounding feat of laying rock walls one above the other to hold the soil on steep slopes is a way of farming said to date back to the Tang Dynasty over one thousand years ago. The practice of terraced farming demonstrates the collective ingenuity of a people who found a way to farm when flat land was not available. An irrigation network was also created to bring precious water to every field. Some of the fields are at such a high elevation that they are often veiled in heavy cloud, mist and rain. The hardy Zhuang, Yao and other ethnic minorities in the region began the back-breaking task of building the terraces hundreds of years ago in response to population pressures.

High on the terraced mountain perch the villages of Longjie (see photo, page 227), which means Dragon's Back, and Ping'an, which means Peace and Tranquility. The villagers' tile-roofed houses are cleverly built from fir

Endless care has created the fertile terraced fields in Longsheng.

logs constructed without the use of nails. The typical houses are three stories high and each level serves a purpose. The top floor is reserved for storing grain, the middle used for living, while the bottom level houses livestock. Small balconies are used for drying laundry, vegetables and grain. There are no chimneys, but the high ceilings provide good ventilation, and the smoke from fires that eventually blacken the wood walls is essential to making their snug homes wind and water resistant and insect proof. The two villages are walled with some stone gateways dating to the Qing Dynasty. Spring water for household use is directed by lengths of bamboo ducts that bring the water right to each family's water storage vessels, which are carved from giant rocks with inscriptions recording the date they were created, some going back to the Qing Dynasty. Decorated stone slabs also serve as pathways between houses. At crossroads are clearly marked stone signs called Jiangjun Jian (general's arrows). The villagers believe that providing directions protects them from disasters.

Huge boulders in the rice paddies bear evidence of what the fields looked like before cultivation (below, left). The bamboo ducts (below, right) bring water to each family's storage vessel.

Among the Yao people there is a particular group called the Hong (Red) Yao, characterized by the red or bright blue clothing the women wear. The Hong Yao are the only group of the Yao where the women have kept the tradition of wearing their hair long. Throughout her life, a woman's hair is cut only twice, at the age of eight before she starts to wear her hair long and at sixteen, as part of an initiation ceremony. Her hairdo also indicates whether she is married or has children.

As in most Chinese villages the communities of the terraces are often composed of families with just one surname. Each village has at least one village elder who is looked up to and respected. This is not a hereditary position, but is an elected one, and the person chosen is judged as someone good for the common welfare and able to create prosperity for the village. These close-knit communities retain many old customs such as wearing traditional costume for celebrations and festivals. Trust is taken for granted in this small world high above the rest of teeming humanity. The beauty of the terraces and the amazing engineering skills required to build and maintain them, and the villages that cling to the mountains, draw many visitors and have long been admired in China.

The fields of Ping'an Village (opposite) are ready for harvest. Grooming their long hair by the creek becomes a photo opportunity (below).

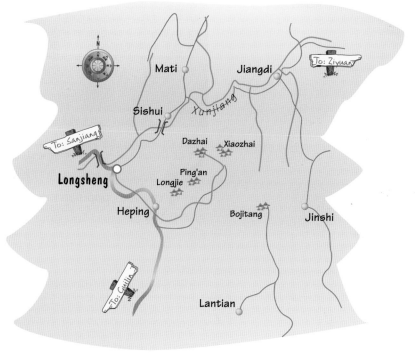

Bamboo Rafting
on the Yulong River

Set in an often misty limestone landscape of pinnacles, sculpted towers and caves, Guilin is a breathtaking city and popular tourist stop on the Lijiang (Li River). The amazing limestone formations that surround the city and its environs were created more than 200 million years ago as an ocean receded from the area. Today jagged hills and spires pop out of paddy fields and line rivers around the city. The unexpected shapes and their reflections in the water delight the many tourists and nature lovers who take a 52-miles (83-km) boat cruise on the Lijiang between Guilin and Yangshuo.

Savvy travelers, however, may prefer to skip jostling on the crowded boats that cruise the river and go to Yangshuo directly, which is an easy 70-minute bus ride. Yangshuo is a smaller and more restful town than Guilin, but it is equally beautiful. It can be used as a base to explore the countryside on a rented bike or on foot. In Shanshui Yuan (Landscape Garden) on the southeast bank of the Lijiang rises Bilianfeng, or Green Lotus Peak, which rewards the climber with spectacular views of the town, its harbor and the river. From Yangshuo Park in the west the views are of the bucolic countryside.

A popular evening ritual in Yangshuo is cormorant

The fisherman and his cormorants (above; opposite) on the Lijiang.

fishing on the river. A fisherman ties a string around the bird's neck to prevent it from swallowing the prey and then has the bird dive for fish in a harness. The bird catches fish in its beak and returns to the bamboo raft with supper for the fisherman's family.

A 5-mile (8-km) bike ride out of Yangshuo goes through gorgeous vistas to Yueliang Shan, or Moon Mountain, which one can climb for a panoramic view of the whole limestone landscape. For experienced spelunkers, there are Heifodong, or Black Buddha Cave, and Shuiyan, or Water Cave, to explore.

Another outing to consider is a bus ride to Xingping, an unspoiled small village with cobblestone streets and stone houses, and a boat ride back to Yangshuo along one of the loveliest sections of the Lijiang. Sights include Jiumahua Shan (the Painted Cliff), Wuzhifeng (Five Fingers Hill) and Huangbutan Daoying (Reflection of Yellow Beach). Walking along the Lijiang is a leisurely way to take in its picturesque beauty. Small towns and villages along the river, such as Yangshuo and Xingping, offer comfortable lodgings for hikers.

But a wonderful outing not to be missed is bamboo

The old stone bridge on the Yulong He (below) is the start of one of the bamboo rafting routes.

The village women still do their laundry in the river.

rafting along the Yulong He (River) into Yangshuo. One can take a bus to Yulong Village, or further upstream to Shangri-La Park. First started in 2001, bamboo rafting along the Yulong has become very popular. The upstream sections flow gently through serene country-side, interrupted only by the excitement of riding over some twenty shallow river dams. The Yulong is a small river, only 7 ft. (2 m) deep and 200 ft. (60 m) at its widest point. The water is so astonishingly clear that fish can be seen swimming in and out of the river-weeds.

Along the river tall and jagged limestone hills shoot up into the sky from rice paddies or citrus fruit orchards. On a lucky day, you can see fish farmers using two long bamboo polls to farm river-weeds used as fish feed. Drinking in the sweet smell of the grass and the citrus flowers and listening to the sound of birds and rippling water is a restful tonic.

Dubbed the Lesser Lijiang, the Yulong runs 27 miles (44 km) before flowing into the Lijiang in Yangshuo. Yulong means "favored by a dragon" and the river is

named for an ancient bridge. According to legend, the bridge, built in the Ming Dynasty, kept collapsing until it was favored by a dragon and became Yulong Bridge. The current bridge, reinforced with new rails in 1870, is one of three ancient bridges on the Yulong River. The other two are Fuli (Rich Village) Bridge and Xiangui (Fairy Osmanthus) Bridge, a single-arch brick bridge that dates back to 1123 of the Song Dynasty. Some of its bricks are inscribed with the dates of the bridge's building and later repairs.

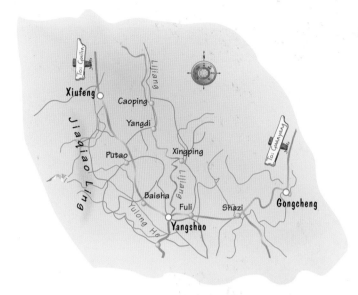

The rice fields and limestone peaks of Qifengzheng (opposite) south of Guilin. The Xiangui Bridge (below) has a 880-year history.

Hakka Earth Towers
in Fujian Province

In a long migration to the southern coastal area from war-ravaged northern China near the end of the Tang Dynasty more than 1,000 years ago, a group of Hakka people, also known as the Jews of China, settled down in coastal Fujian Province. Their sense of insecurity brought them to several remote mountain valleys in Fujian. These northern migrants created one of the most unique architectures in Chinese history. What they built is known today as earth towers, a ring-shaped, self-contained housing complex, resembling a circular fortress.

For generations these towers have shielded Hakka people, their families and their living quarters against invasion. Japanese pirates who wreaked havoc along Chinese coastal provinces during the Ming Dynasty in the fifteenth century often skipped the Hakka earth tower areas in search of easier targets.

The tower itself is comparable to a Western-style castle whose sole entrance opens to a huge open-air central courtyard with views open to all the rooms built surrounding the yard. The tower can also take a variety of shapes: rectangular, semi-circular and square. A small earth tower rises up two stories and has one ring and more than twenty-one rooms. Bigger constructions can go as high as five stories, with multiple rings and as many as fifty-eight rooms. The inner rings are often shaped like a rice bowl, with the height of inner rings lower than the outside rings. The Hakka people use these rooms for multiple functions, as bathrooms, kitchens, family shrines, as well as schools, warehouses and theaters.

Earth towers spread mainly across three counties in Fujian Province: Yongding, Nanjing and Pinghe. The most renowned earth tower, the two-ringed Zhencheng Tower built in 1912, is in Yongding County.

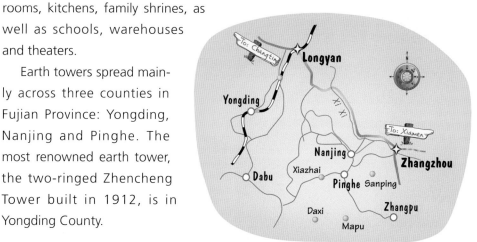

The Hakka earth towers resemble a circular fortress (outer walls on opposite page, interior structures on pages 238–239).

The *Ta'an Creek Valley,*
Home of the Gaoshans

From its source in the Hsuehshan (Snow Mountains) in central Taiwan, the Ta'an Chi (Creek) converges with several other rivers and mountain creeks before entering the Taiwan Strait in Taichung. A 13-mile (20-km) section of the river from Meiyuan (Plum Garden) Village in Miaoli County to Hsuehshankung (Snow Mountain Basin) in Taichung County broadens into an open valley. The valley is inhabited mostly by the Atayal, one of the groups of the Gaoshan people in Taiwan. Eight different tribes of the Atayal live on the mountain slopes on both sides of the Ta'an Chi in this valley. Despite rapid economic development in the rest of Taiwan, the Atayals still make their living growing rice, fruit and mushrooms or planting fir and bamboo trees.

The water level of the Ta'an Chi fluctuates during the year. During the rainy season, the river is about 1,000 yd.

The suspended cable bridge stretches over the Ta'an Chi (opposite). Atayal women dance in their festive red costumes (below).

(1,000 m) wide. The currents are so rapid that boats cannot safely ferry across. In the dry season, however, the river is one-sixth of its normal size and becomes a shallow creek in the middle of an almost dry riverbed. Some farmers use the exposed riverbed to grow rice. The river used to be crossed by a simple bamboo bridge, put up haphazardly for the dry season or a suspended cable bridge, part of an old Hsiangpi Trail, that connected Hsiangpi Village with other villages in the valley. Nowadays there is a more permanent bridge downstream from the long-abandoned cable bridge. Not too far downstream from the Hsiangpi Village is Hsuehshankung, set in an area known as Taohuaku (Peach Blossom Valley). In early spring when the peach trees blossom, the whole valley becomes a sea of pink flowers.

While Ta'an Creek Valley is fairly isolated from the outside world, a surprising number of churches have been built in the villages. They are of different denominations ranging from Evangelical to Catholic, and testify to the early influence of Christianity in this territory.

*H*unghsiang
Hot Springs and Tiepilun Gorge

Though commonly referred to as only one place, Hunghsiang Hot Springs are actually situated in two neighboring villages separated by a valley stream. Hunghsiang in the Fahsiang Village and Hot Spring in the Lihsin Village are connected by a suspension bridge. The inhabitants are mostly of the Gaoshan ethnic group. Tucked in the secluded valley in the upper reaches of Peikang Chi (North Harbor Creek), this isolated area is a retreat where one can still enjoy mountain scenery in its pristine state.

Hunghsiang Hot Springs are part of a secluded spa area in Hohuan Shan, a mountain range with seven peaks over 10,000 ft. (3,000 m) above sea level. The origin of the hot springs lies in the Spa Village under a suspension bridge. The water is a type of weak carbon acidic springs with a temperature of 145°F (63°C). It can be an intoxicating experience to soak in the outdoor bathing pools while enjoying the sight of maple leaves in autumn and listening to birds in the trees. While fruit, mushrooms, rice and vegetables are the major produce here; raising fish, especially the North American rainbow trout, is very popular as well. Fish farms are scattered all

The cloud-filled valley seen from Tayuling (opposite) is in the same area as the Hunghsiang Hot Springs (below).

The Tiepilun Waterfall cascades down in several steps (left). A path traverses the Hohuan Shan (opposite).

throughout the high-altitude region.

Apart from enjoying the hot springs, one can explore the neighboring Tiepilun Gorge about 3 miles (5 km) away. Together with Hunghsiang Hot Springs, Tiepilun is ranked one of the two best destinations of Jenaihsiang, Nantou County, the only county in Taiwan without a coastline. The Tiepilun Gorge lies in the mid-stream section of Tiepilun Stream, which originates from the southern slope of Paikoutashan (Mt. Great White Dog). With a narrow riverbed flowing over a terraced terrain, its rapid current is a rare phenomenon in Taiwan, as is the Tiepilun Waterfall with its gushing torrents that rush into a deep pool 16 ft. (5 m) below.

Index

PICTURE CREDITS & ACKNOWLEDGMENTS

Front Cover: Sun Moon Mountain. Photo by Yang Xing-Bin.

Back Cover: Lijiang, Guifeng, Longsheng. Photo by Zhong Jun-Feng, Li Ya-Shi (1 & 3).

Panorama Stock Photos Co., Ltd.
www.quanjing.com

2-3, 8-9, 14, 16, 21, 28-29, 32, 38-39, 40, 41, 42-43, 45, 46-47, 48-49, 50, 52, 53, 59, 60-61, 62-63, 66, 68-69, 70-71, 72, 73, 75, 80-81, 82, 86, 87, 90, 94-95, 99, 104-105, 106-107, 108, 115, 119, 120, 122, 124-125, 130-131, 136-137, 138-139, 140-141, 154-155, 163, 164-165, 170, 171, 172, 174-175, 177, 178-179, 179 (top), 183, 188-189, 194-195, 196-197, 202-203, 203 (bottom), 204-205, 206, 207, 208-209, 216 (top), (bottom), 224-225, 231

Photocome.com
www.photocome.com

11 Xiao Dian-Chang. 27 (bottom) Liu Zhao-Ming; (top) Liu Zhao-Ming. 29 (bottom) Liu Zhao-Ming. 30 Liu Zhao-Ming. 43 Xie Yong. 150 Lin Yu-Song. 198 Wu Lü-Ming. 201 Xie Yong. 212 Wu Dong-Jun. 213 You Ma-Cai.

Guangzhou Integrated Image Co., Ltd.
www.fotoe.com

13 Liu Suo. 22 Xiao Dian-Chang. 31 An Ge. 35 Chen Huai. 64 (top) Song Shi-Jing. 67 Wu Ping-Guan. 68 (top) Zhang Wen-Cheng. 74 Yang Xing-Bin. 76 (left) Shi Bao-Xiu. (right) Chen Huai. 77 Li Jiang-Shu. 78 Li Quan-Jü. 79 Luo Xiao-Yun. 100 Li Wen.

101 Shui Xiao-Jie. 102 Li Wen. 103 Li Wen. 117 (top) Li Jiang-Shu. 152 Ar Cun. 180 Ma Wen-Tian. 190 Shui Xiao-Jie. 199 (top) Wang Zhi-Zhong. 200 Luo Xiao-Yun. 202 (top) Liao Wen-Ying. 215 (right) Wu Lü-Ming.

China Online Photo
www.colphoto.com

10 Wang Xue-Lin. 12 Chen Yong-Jie. 64 (bottom) Shao Ru-Lin. 65 Yang Gui-Fang. 109 Shang Zu-Yu. 116 Wang Xue-Feng. 181 Yin Nan. 193 Chu Tian. 194 Reporters.

Bejing Spark Culture Developing Co., Ltd.

18 Ding Xiao-Min. 19 Ding Xiao-Min. 24 Hao Peng. 25 Hao Peng. 26 Zhang Hai. 51 Chen Zheng. 112-113 Ye Jun. 113 Ye Jun.

Jiangxi Gold Picture Co., Ltd.
www.goldenpicture.com

158 Jin Long. 160 Jin Long. 161 Jin Long. 162 Jin Long. 165 (bottom) Peng Wen-Hua. 166 Zhong Jun-Feng. 167 (top) Zhong Jun-Feng; (bottom) Zhong Jun-Feng.

China Tourism

15 Chan Yat-Nin. 17 Yang Yan-Kang. 23 Kit Chu. 55 Chan Yat-Nin. 70 (bottom) Jackie Tsang. 71 (top) Shi Bao-Xiu. 96 Dianna Lau. 97 Zaxi Cideng. 98 Xie Guang-Hui. 117 (bottom) Hu Yan-Bin. 121 Dianna Lau. 148 Zhou Xiao-Yin. 151 Zhou Xiao-Yin. 156 China Tourism.

Others

1 Li Ya-Shi. 33 Zhou Zhi-Ping. 34 Zhou Zhi-

Ping. 36-37 Zhou Zhi-Ping. 54 Jin Ling. 56 Jin Ling. 57 Jin Ling. 84 Liu Tao. 85 Jin Ling. 88 Liu tao. 89 Liu tao. 91 Liu tao. 92-93 Liu tao. 110 Liu Tao. 111 Li Meng. 118 Jin Ling. 123 L. Chen. 126 L. Chen. 127 L. Chen. 128 L. Chen. 129 L. Chen. 132 L. Chen. 133 L. Chen. 134 L. Chen. 135 L. Chen. 141 Xiao Xian-Tai. 142 Zhou Zhi-Ping. 143 Jin Ling. 144 Jin Ling. 145 L. Chen. 146 (top) Jin Ling; (bottom) L. Chen. 147 L. Chen. 157 L. Chen. 159 Loh Wing-Cheung. 168 Jin Ling. 169 Jin Ling. 182 Loh Wing-Cheung. 184 Zheng Chun-Sheng. 185 Zheng Chun-Sheng. 186 Zheng Chun-Sheng. 187 Zheng Chun-Sheng. 191 Jin Ling. 192 Xiao Xian-Tai. 199 (bottom) Xiao Xian-Tai. 210 (left) Margaret Loh; (right) Margaret Loh. 211 Margaret Loh. 214 Yao Yu-Liang. 215 (left) Yao Yu-Liang. 217 Li Ya-Shi. 218 L. Chen. 219 L. Chen. 220 (left) Li Ya-Shi; (right) L. Chen. 221 L. Chen. 222 Yao Yu-Liang. 223 Li Ya-Shi. 226 (left) L. Chen; (right) L. Chen. 227 L. Chen. 228 L. Chen. 229 L. Chen. 230 Li Ya-Shi. 232 L. Chen. 233 L. Chen. 234 Li Ya-Shi. 235 L. Chen. 236 Lin Jiang-Sheng. 238-239 Lin Jiang-Sheng. 240 Hilit. 241 Hilit. 242 Hilit. 243 Hilit. 244 Hilit. 245 Hilit.

The publishers wish to express their gratitude to the following people for translating, contributing and editing some of the text in this book:
Mirror Fung; Sarah Xie; Betsy J. Kelly; Shu-Ching Jean Chen